ANN KELLY
MARILYNS CHRISTMAS PRESENT

No need to
to
Cook
Book

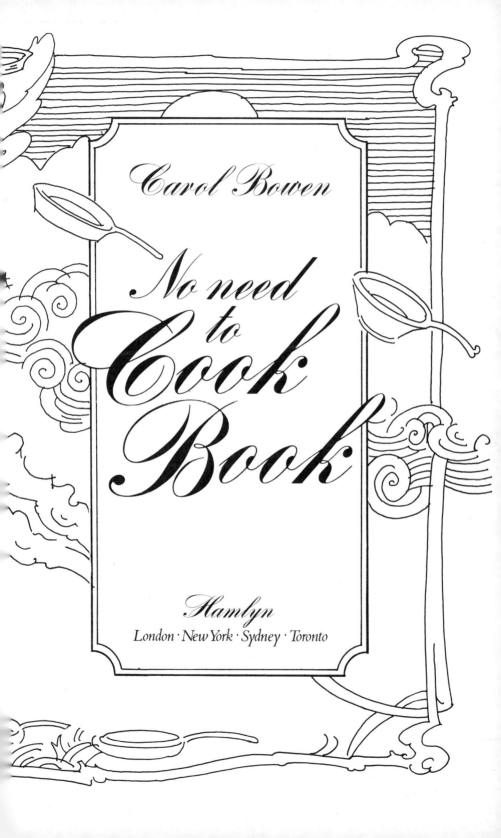

Carol Bowen

No need to Cook Book

Hamlyn
London · New York · Sydney · Toronto

For Peter "who hasn't had a cooked meal in months"

Photography by Paul Williams
Line illustrations by Robin Laurie

Published by
The Hamlyn Publishing Group Limited
London . New York . Sydney . Toronto
Astronaut House, Feltham, Middlesex, England
© Copyright
The Hamlyn Publishing Group Limited 1981
ISBN 0 600 32241 6

Phototypeset by Photocomp Limited, Birmingham
Printed in Italy

Contents

Useful Facts and Figures

Notes on metrication
In this book quantities are given in metric and Imperial measures. Exact conversion from Imperial to metric measures does not usually give very convenient working quantities and so the metric measures have been rounded off into units of 25 grams. The table below shows the recommended equivalents.

Ounces	Approx g to nearest whole figure	Recommended conversion to nearest unit of 25	Ounces	Approx g to nearest whole figure	Recommended conversion to nearest unit of 25
1	28	25	11	312	300
2	57	50	12	340	350
3	85	75	13	368	375
4	113	100	14	396	400
5	142	150	15	425	425
6	170	175	16 (1 lb)	454	450
7	198	200	17	482	475
8	227	225	18	510	500
9	255	250	19	539	550
10	283	275	20 ($1\frac{1}{4}$ lb)	567	575

Note: When converting quantities over 20 oz first add the appropriate figures in the centre column, then adjust to the nearest unit of 25. As a general guide, 1 kg (1000 g) equals 2.2 lb or about 2 lb 3 oz. This method of conversion gives good results in nearly all cases, although in certain pastry and cake recipes a more accurate conversion is necessary to produce a balanced recipe.

Liquid measures The millilitre has been used in this book and the following table gives a few examples.

Imperial	Approx ml to nearest whole figure	Recommended ml	Imperial	Approx ml to nearest whole figure	Recommended ml
$\frac{1}{4}$ pint	142	150 ml	1 pint	567	600 ml
$\frac{1}{2}$ pint	283	300 ml	$1\frac{1}{2}$ pints	851	900 ml
$\frac{3}{4}$ pint	425	450 ml	$1\frac{3}{4}$ pints	992	1000 ml (1 litre)

Spoon measures All spoon measures given in this book are level unless otherwise stated.

Can sizes At present, cans are marked with the exact (usually to the nearest whole number) metric equivalent of the Imperial weight of the contents, so we have followed this practice when giving can sizes.

Note: When making any of the recipes in this book, only follow one set of measures as they are not interchangeable.

Notes for American and Australian users

In America the 8-oz measuring cup is used. In Australia metric measures are now used in conjunction with the standard 250-ml measuring cup. The Imperial pint, used in Britain and Australia, is 20 fl oz, while the American pint is 16 fl oz. It is important to remember that the Australian tablespoon differs from both the British and American tablespoons; the table below gives a comparison. The British standard tablespoon, which has been used throughout this book, holds 17.7 ml, the American 14.2 ml, and the Australian 20 ml. A teaspoon holds approximately 5 ml in all three countries.

British	American	Australian	British	American	Australian
1 teaspoon	1 teaspoon	1 teaspoon	3½ table-spoons	4 table-spoons	3 table-spoons
1 table-spoon	1 table-spoon	1 table-spoon	4 table-spoons	5 table-spoons	3½ table-spoons
2 table-spoons	3 table-spoons	2 table-spoons			

An Imperial/American guide to solid and liquid measures

Imperial	American	Imperial	American
Solid measures		**Liquid measures**	
1 lb butter or margarine	2 cups	¼ pint liquid	⅔ cup liquid
1 lb flour	4 cups	½ pint	1¼ cups
1 lb granulated or castor sugar	2 cups	¾ pint	2 cups
1 lb icing sugar	3 cups	1 pint	2½ cups
8 oz rice	1 cup	1½ pints	3¾ cups
		2 pints	5 cups (2½ pints)

American terms

The list below gives some American equivalents or substitutes for terms and ingredients used in this book.

Equipment and terms	Ingredients
British/American	*British/American*
clingfilm/saran wrap	black olives/ripe olives
cocktail stick/toothpick	celery stick/celery stalk
foil/aluminium foil	chocolate, plain/chocolate, semi-sweet
greaseproof paper/waxed paper	courgettes/zucchini
gut fish/clean fish	crystallised and glacé fruits/candied fruits
mince/grind	digestive biscuits/graham crackers
muslin/cheesecloth	freshly opened oysters/freshly shucked oysters
packet/package	gelatine/gelatin
piping bag/pastry bag	green grapes/white grapes
polythene/plastic	lemon jelly/lemon-flavoured gelatin
top and tail/stem and head	raisins, seedless/raisins, seeded
	soured cream/dairy sour cream
	spring onion/scallion
	sugar, icing/confectioners' sugar
	sultanas/seedless white raisins
	yogurt, natural/yogurt, plain

Introduction

If, like me, you experience occasions when you really don't want to cook, simply can't risk disaster cooking a new dish or find that cold fare is the order of the day – then you'll find this book invaluable.

I always seem to face a busy new day with good intentions of preparing a steaming hot evening meal – only to run out of time; get cold feet during the last minutes of preparing what promises to be a stunning but time-inflexible hot soufflé and resort to a time and flavour tested favourite cold recipe that I know will work; and occasionally strike lucky when a day at home proves to be wonderfully sunny and we can eat out of doors!

Such occasions seem to happen with such regularity that it hasn't seemed too difficult to put together my favourite no-cook recipes to suit every meal occasion and using cold food standbys like fruit, vegetables, dairy foods and nuts, and smoked or cured fish, meat and poultry. Teamed with some interesting new ideas for raw meat, fish and eggs, which you may not have tried before, I hope you will enjoy many a no-need-to-cook meal.

Carol Bowen

No-Cook Know-How

Simply forgetting about cooking, which this book happily does, doesn't mean, however, forgetting about all the other procedures concerned with good food preparation. Indeed food buying and preparation may take on a new significance with no-need-to-cook dishes since they are the only 'factors at risk to the perfectly prepared dish. No-Cook Know-How is what it is all about and it continues on the following pages. Armed with such advice and hints on buying foods of good quality, storing those foods in the best possible way and preparing them for tasty results, will inevitably lead to a fine repertoire of dishes that not only do not require cooking but will delight your family and friends. Nothing could really be simpler!

Buying for Quality

Quite obviously, it is extremely important when eating food, raw or uncooked, to choose produce that is fresh and at the peak of good quality. A reliable and regular supplier of meat and fish will usually put paid to any doubts of this nature and if you follow the preparation procedures for storing and cleaning food on the following pages, there should not be any fear of eating raw uncooked food. Since such food is only lightly prepared and does not undergo cooking to change its nature or structure, it is of particular importance to buy the very best quality food that you can afford – invest the fuel savings you make on buying tip-top quality food and you will be repaid with extra flavour and nutritional benefits. Poor quality fruit and vegetables cannot be disguised with no-cook recipes.

The days have gone by when a regular local supplier could be relied upon to monitor the freshness and quality of the food you purchase – today it is down to basic good foodkeeping. From the checklist below, try to memorise some of the sound characteristics that indicate a good buy and a poor one and you will have the basics and key to a good many meals at hand.

Top Fruit

Top fruit or tree fruit includes such fruits as apples, pears, stone fruits such as cherries, plums, peaches, nectarines and finally nuts. It is essential to only buy enough of these fruits to last a few days as such fruits do not keep for long at room temperatures. Apples and pears will store for a couple of weeks if they are kept in a cool, airy cellar or larder, but all stone fruit, with the exception of plums and nuts, are best eaten on the day of purchase.

Apples Look for apples with smooth skins and avoid any with brownish bruises.

Apricots Buy firm fruits, avoiding any with bruised or squashy, brown skins.

Peaches Avoid any peaches which have split or those with bruised skins and brown or soft spots.

Pears Pears bruise easily and should be handled with care; they are best bought before fully ripe and left in the airing cupboard for 2–3 days. Ripe pears will yield gently when pressed at the stalk end.

Plums Dessert plums should be firm to the touch, with a bloom on the skin; they are often sold under ripe and can be kept in a cool larder for 1–3 days before serving.

Chestnuts Look for shiny brown fruits and avoid those that look brown and shrivelled.

Hazelnuts Choose ripe fresh nuts that have firm, not shrivelled husks.

Walnuts The brown shells of walnuts should have a faint, damp sheen. Avoid any which rattle, as they will be dry and shrivelled.

Soft Fruit

Strawberries, raspberries and currants are all soft fruits which are best used on the day or purchase. All soft fruit, with the exception of gooseberries, leave stains on the bottom of their container; so avoid buying any in badly stained containers as the fruits are bound to be mushy and often mouldy. As soon as possible after buying, tip the berries carefully on to a plate, pick out any mouldy berries and set the remainder well apart on a tray until serving.

Citrus Fruit

As all citrus fruits have a fairly thick skin, it is sometimes difficult to tell the condition of the fruit. In general, all fruits should have a bright, taut and slightly moist skin with a definite aroma. So avoid buying citrus fruits that are dry looking or any that have soft indentations or blemishes to the skin.

Citrus fruits store fairly well. Lemons and grapefruit can be kept in the vegetable box of the refrigerator for 1–2 weeks, and other types can be stored in a cool larder for about 1 week. They must, however, be used before the skins shrivel. Before cutting or serving the fruits, they should be rolled between the palms or on a flat surface to get an even distribution of juice within the fruit.

Vegetables

Ideally, vegetables should come straight from the field or garden into the kitchen. Though this is seldom possible, there are many clues to the freshness or age of vegetables in the shops. Choose crisp and firm vegetables rather than hard ones, and avoid small vegetables which are probably immature and therefore lacking in flavour. Over-large vegetables, on the other hand, are usually coarse.

White Fish

Fresh fish can be recognised by its firm flesh, clear, full and shiny eyes, bright red gills and clean smell. Steaks, cutlets and fillets should have firm, closely packed flakes; any with a fibrous or watery appearance are stale. Fish with flesh that has a blue or green tinge is almost certainly not fresh – on flat fish, this is most apparent on the dark side.

Oily Fish

When buying oily fish, look for fresh fish with firm, even-textured flesh, clear, full and shiny eyes, bright red gills and a clean smell. Generally, there are two methods by which oily fish can be smoked; hot smoking, in which the temperature in the smoking kiln is raised sufficiently to cook the fish which then requires no cooking prior to eating. This is the kind of fish that is bought at most delicatessens. Cold-smoking, however, usually implies that the fish must be cooked further in the kitchen before eating and has not been used in the recipes in this book. Hot-smoked fish must be eaten soon after curing; cold-smoked fish will keep longer if lightly wrapped in clingfilm and stored in the refrigerator.

Shellfish

Crab When buying crab, shake it lightly, it should feel heavy but with no sound of water inside.
Mussels Almost always served cooked but occasionally sold ready cooked for use in salads etc. Choose firm, unbroken mussels with good amber colour.
Oysters These highly prized molluscs are usually eaten raw, but may be cooked. When buying, choose oysters with shells that are firmly closed or shut when tapped. Oysters must be absolutely fresh and should be opened just before serving.
Prawns Sold ready cooked. Look for prawns with a firm-textured flesh and bright pink colour.

Meat

Beef The best beef comes from young animals, but even so it must, after slaughtering, be matured or 'hung' at low temperatures to tenderise the meat with the minimum loss of weight and to improve its keeping qualities. On properly hung beef, the lean meat should be plum-red in colour and slightly moist. Very bright, red meat denotes that the meat has not been hung sufficiently and therefore is not tender. Dark red, lean and sinewy beef indicates cuts from an animal not of prime quality and likely to be tough. Quality beef should have a good outside covering of fat, creamy to pale yellow and of firm texture. The bones should be shiny and pinkish with a blue tinge. There should be little or no gristle.
Lamb British lamb varies in colour according to the age and breed of the animal. Meat from a young lamb is usually pale pink; red meat comes from an older animal. Any fat should be creamy-white, not oily or yellow – a yellowish tinge shows excessive age. Look for a piece of lamb with flesh that is pliable to the touch, not hard or wrinkled. A blue tinge in any bones also indicates that the animal is young.
Ham Smoked or cooked ham, usually sold sliced, should look fresh with white fat and pink flesh.

Cheese

Whether you are buying a whole cheese or a ready-cut, pre-packed piece, avoid anything which looks too dry, too hard, too soft and, especially if pre-packed, cheese which looks as though it has sweated. Suspect any pieces of cheese, particularly the 'hard-pressed' varieties such as English Cheddar, Gloucester or Leicester, which show numerous cracks running in from the edges, or which have a marked difference in colour between the centre and the edge. These are sure signs that it is not fresh and has started to dry out.

Once a cheese has matured it does not improve with keeping, especially when cut, so buy from day to day if possible, rather than stocking up with several weeks supply. Ideally, cheese should be kept in a container in a cool larder. A plastic container would be ideal. But if this is not possible, the refrigerator is the next best place. Take any cheese from the refrigerator at least one hour before serving so that it is allowed to reach room temperature.

When choosing soft cheeses, choose a cheese that is soft right through to the centre for the perfect flavour – avoid those with a chalky white line through them since they are definitely under ripe.

Eggs

Eggs are probably one of the most useful of foods since there is no waste on them apart from the shell. Test an egg for freshness by lowering it into a bowl of water. If it lies on its side it is quite fresh; if it stands on end it is less fresh; and if it floats to the top it is stale and possibly bad. When broken, a fresh egg smells pleasant, the yolk is round and firm and the white evenly distributed. A stale egg usually has a slight smell, and spreads out thinly when broken.

Eggs kept at normal room temperature, about 18°C (65°F), will stay fresh for about 10 days, but they are better stored in a cool larder. In the refrigerator they will keep for as long as 2 months. Remove the eggs from the refrigerator at least 45 minutes before using.

Separated eggs should be stored in the refrigerator, in separate covered containers. Pour a thin layer of milk or water over the yolks to prevent them hardening. Yolks can be stored for 4 days, but whites should not be kept for more than 2–3 days.

Pointers to Good Preparation

No-cook recipes mean simply that – but they still do involve preparation and some that must be extremely thorough because of the no-cooking principle. Whether it be cleaning fruit and vegetables, chopping meat or filleting fish, absolute cleanliness is a must. Attention paid to the details of preparation will also add to your reputation as a 'cook' so follow the advice below for five-star prepared food for no-cook feasts.

Fish

Fish is sold fresh, frozen, salted from the barrel, smoked, pickled or canned. Flat fish is often sold whole or filleted, while round fish may also be sold as steaks or cutlets. Shellfish are generally sold ready cooked and often prepared, the exceptions being mussels and oysters which are almost always bought alive.

It is essential to use fish on the day it is bought and as a general guide allow about 175 g/6 oz per person. Fishmongers will generally clean and fillet any fish you buy but if this has not been done, a few simple preparations are required: —

Preparation of Fish Unwrap the fish as soon as possible and if it has to be stored in the refrigerator for any length of time, wrap it in plastic clingfilm or foil to prevent the smell from spreading to other food. Preparation of fish includes scaling, cleaning, skinning and sometimes filleting: —

Scaling Cover a wooden board with several sheets of newspaper. Lay the fish on the paper and, holding it by the tail, scrape away the scales from the tail towards the head, using the blunt edge of a knife. Rinse the scales off under cold water.

Cleaning Once scaled, the fish must be cleaned, or gutted. This process is determined by the shape of the fish – in round fish, the entrails lie in the belly, in flat fish they lie in a cavity behind the head.

For *round fish*, slit the fish with a sharp knife along the belly, from behind the gills to just above the tail. Scrape out and discard the entrails. Rinse the fish under cold running water and, with a little salt, gently rub away any black skin inside the cavity. Using a sharp knife, remove the head and tail from the fish then, using a sharp knife or scissors, cut off the lower fins on either side of the body and the gills below the head. Small round fish, such as sardines, smelts and sprats, need less preparation. Wipe the fish with a damp cloth, cut off the heads just below the gills, leaving the tails intact. Squeeze out the entrails.

Flat fish should have a semi-circular slit made just behind the head, on the dark skin side. This opens up the cavity which contains the entrails. Scrape these out and wash the fish. Cut off the fins then skin, if liked.

Skinning Yet again, the method of skinning depends upon the type of fish. For *round fish*, loosen the skin around the head with a sharp knife and then gently draw the skin down towards the tail. Cut the tail and skin off and repeat on the other side of the fish. When skinning *flat fish* lay the fish, dark skin uppermost, on a board. Make a slit across the skin just above the tail. Slip your thumb into the slit and gently loosen the skin. Holding the fish firmly by the tail, pull the skin quickly towards the head (dip your fingers in salt to get a better grip). Cut the head off. Remove any white skin on the other side in the same way.

Filleting and Boning The fish can now be cut into portions. Fillets of both round and flat fish are popular for no-cook recipes.

Round fish should first be cut along the backbone, working towards the tail. Insert the knife blade at a slight angle to the bone and, keeping the sharp edge towards the tail, gently ease the flesh from the bone with slicing movements. Continue cutting in line with the backbone, until the whole fillet is freed. Open out the fish and cut off the fillet at the tail. With the tip of the knife, ease off the backbone to reveal the other fillet, and cut off the tail.

A large *flat fish* will yield four small fillets, two from each side. Lay the fish, dark skin up, on a board and with a sharp knife cut off the fins. Make the first cut along the backbone, working from the head towards the tail. Then make a semi-circular cut, just below the head, through half the thickness of the fish. Slant the knife against the backbone, and with short sharp strokes of the knife, separate the left fillet from the bone. Make a thick cut just above the tail and remove the fillet. Turn the fish round and remove the right fillet in the same way. Turn the fish over and remove the fillets on the other side.

Meat

Meat is generally bought fresh, frozen, chilled or ready-cooked. Frozen meat is generally sold thawed, but if it is chilled or frozen when purchased, it should be allowed to thaw thoroughly at room temperature before preparing. Fresh meat will keep for 2–3 days in the refrigerator. Remove the wrapping paper as soon as possible after purchase and wipe the meat with a damp cloth to remove any blood or sawdust. Place the meat on a clean dish, wrap it loosely in plastic clingfilm and store in the refrigerator. Cooked meats should be eaten as quickly as possible after purchase and should be stored in the refrigerator until required.

Vegetables

For food value and good flavour, you cannot beat fresh vegetables. If they have to be stored, keep them in a cool airy place, such as a larder or in the vegetable compartment of the refrigerator. However, there are certain fruits and vegetables that should not be stored together. Carrots stored next to apples will take on a bitter taste; and potatoes will quickly spoil if they are stored with onions. Cut the leaves from root vegetables before storing, to prevent the sap rising from the roots.

Choose vegetables that are crisp and firm and prepare them by thoroughly washing and if necessary, scrubbing with a brush. Do not soak vegetables at any stage during their preparation because their mineral salts and vitamins are soluble in water. Because the most nutritious part of root vegetables and onions lie just under the skin, only a thin outer layer should be peeled away with a knife. If the vegetables are young, just scrape them lightly.

Vegetables may be used whole or may be cut up for no-cook recipes. Either way, follow the procedure for cleaning as above. To cut vegetables, use a sharp kitchen knife. When slicing, do not lift the point of the knife away from the chopping board but use it as a pivot. Keep the wrist flexible and raise the knife just above the vegetable before chopping down again. Guide the knife with a forefinger down the back of the blade.

Some vegetables, cabbages for example, may be merely halved and shredded before use; but most can be prepared using one of the following methods of preparation: —

Slicing Cut vegetables into narrow rounds or slices and divide these into sticks or strips, if liked.

Dicing Slice vegetables lengthways into sticks; then cut these across into small cubes.

Shredding Cut thin slivers from the sides of a vegetable, such as cabbage, which has been halved or quartered. Slice evenly and rhythmically, always bringing the knife just above the vegetable before pressing down again.

Rounds Cut the vegetable crossways to get thick, round slices.

Chopping Cut the vegetables finely or roughly as required.

Fruit

Fresh fruit makes delicious eating on its own without any cooking. With crop-spraying so widespread in modern fruit farming, it is essential that all soft fruit should be washed in running water before serving. Apart from soft fruits, such as blackberries, most fruit will keep in good condition for up to 1 week if stored in a refrigerator.

Eggs

Eggs are probably one of the most useful of the no-cook aids. They are used as an emulsifying agent in mayonnaise and salad dressings and as a raising agent in soufflés, mousses and other aerated mixtures. Often the eggs have to be separated and beaten for best results – preparation that if carefully followed, gives excellent faultless results: —

Separating Eggs Knock the egg sharply against the rim of a bowl or cup to break the shell in half. Slip the yolk from one half-shell to the other until all the white has drained into the bowl, then slide the yolk into another bowl.

Beating Eggs Whole eggs should be beaten vigorously, turning them over with upward movements, using a fork, whisk or electric beater. Beating draws in air and so increases the volume of the eggs; the biggest volume is obtained from eggs beaten in a warm room. Beaten eggs must be used immediately before they lose air.

When mixing egg yolks and sugar, beat the yolks first, then add the sugar and continue beating until the mixture drops in broad ribbons.

Egg whites, beaten to a stiff but not dry foam, are used for soufflés and meringues. Use a spotlessly clean and dry bowl, of a shape which keeps the whisk in constant contact with the egg whites.

Folding in Egg Whites Pile the beaten egg whites on top of the mixture and, with a metal spoon, draw part of the mixture from the bottom of the bowl over the whites. Incorporate all the whites carefully so that they do not lose their air content.

No-Cook Nutrition

Sadly, there is no firm rule that says raw food is nutritionally better than cooked food. That is, of course, if the food is cooked properly. Badly cooked food runs the risk of losing valuable vitamins and minerals especially those that are water or fat soluble. Some minerals are also unstable with heat and can be reduced dramatically. No-cooking preserves such nutrients and does not put in doubt their availability or concentration.

Do not risk their availability by preparing wrongly. For example, do not leave fruit and vegetables in water for long periods – they can lose those valuable water soluble vitamins simply by soaking as well as by cooking in water. Do not store food in dry or sunny conditions and do not peel vegetables or fruit too thickly – some of the highest concentrations of vitamins and minerals lie just under the skin of food. Prepared carefully, no-cook or raw food should have the highest level of possible nutrients that a food can offer.

Soups and Appetisers

Soups and appetisers play the same primary role; served at the start of a meal, they excite the palate and stimulate the appetite for the courses that follow. Easy work when you have classic Gazpacho – a beguiling combination of peppers, onion, garlic and tomatoes topped with more of the same and crispy croûtons, or Kipper Cocktail made with flaked kipper fillets, crunchy apples and celery in a piquant sauce, on the menu.

For the hostess, cold soups and appetisers that do not require cooking are a bonus – they leave her free to concentrate on the main course and can generally be made well ahead. Most, however, are substantial enough to cope with a light lunch or supper on their own and will prove endlessly useful as quick and easy to prepare emergency food.

During the winter months, when hot food is the order of the day, serve soups, hors d'oeuvres and appetisers of the cold variety with piping hot bread or hot water biscuits to ring the changes in what might otherwise be a predictable diet of steaming soups and casseroles.

Gazpacho

(Illustrated on page 33)

A classic Spanish soup, cold Gazpacho makes a
refreshing summer lunch served with croûtons, small bowls of
chopped olives, cucumbers, peppers and onion. Each guest
sprinkles his own soup with a little of these accompaniments.
The soup can be served puréed or chunky – if your prefer a
chunky version, simply do not purée the vegetables.

3 small slices brown bread, cut into 2.5-cm/1-inch cubes
600 ml/1 pint canned tomato juice
2 garlic cloves, finely chopped
½ cucumber, peeled and finely chopped
1 green pepper, seeds removed and finely chopped
1 large onion, peeled and finely chopped
1 red pepper, seeds removed and finely chopped
675 g/1½ lb tomatoes, peeled, seeds removed and finely chopped
4½ tablespoons olive oil
2 tablespoons red wine vinegar
½ teaspoon salt
¼ teaspoon freshly ground black pepper
¼ teaspoon dried marjoram
¼ teaspoon dried basil
ice cubes (optional)
GARNISH
croûtons
chopped olives
chopped cucumber
chopped green and red peppers
chopped onion

Place the bread cubes in a mixing bowl and pour over the tomato
juice. Leave to soak for 5 minutes, then squeeze them to extract the
juice. Transfer to a large mixing bowl. Reserve the tomato juice.

Add the garlic, cucumber, green pepper, onion, red pepper and
tomatoes to the soaked bread cubes and stir to mix. Purée the
vegetables in a blender or by passing through a fine sieve or by
pounding in a mortar. Stir in the reserved tomato juice.

Add the oil, vinegar, salt, pepper, marjoram and basil to the purée
and mix well. The soup should be the consistency of single cream so
add more tomato juice if necessary.

Turn the soup into a deep tureen and chill for at least 1 hour. Just
before serving, stir the soup well and float ice cubes on the surface, if
used. Serve garnished with croûtons, chopped olives, cucumber,
peppers and onion. SERVES 4

Lebanese Cucumber Soup

There are many variations for this popular Middle Eastern cold soup but this is a very tasty version and so simple to make. It should be served icy cold topped with a few floating pink shrimps.

1 large or 2 small cucumbers
300 ml/½ pint single cream
150 ml/¼ pint natural yogurt
1 clove garlic
2 tablespoons tarragon vinegar
salt and freshly ground black pepper
2 tablespoons finely chopped fresh mint
GARNISH
1 tablespoon finely chopped cocktail gherkins
mint sprigs
12 cooked shrimps, shelled

Wash and dry the cucumber. Without peeling, coarsely grate into a bowl. Stir in the cream and the yogurt. Peel and crush the garlic and add to the cucumber mixture with the tarragon vinegar. Season to taste then stir in the chopped mint. Chill for at least 1 hour before serving garnished with chopped gherkins, mint sprigs and shelled shrimps. SERVES 4–6

Cold Apricot Soup

Cold fruit soups were, and often still are, served at the beginning of the main Christmas day meal in many parts of Hungary and Austria. More often today, they are served as a cool starter to a summery meal.

225 g/8 oz fresh apricots
juice of ½ lemon
600 ml/1 pint dry white wine
50 g/2 oz castor sugar

Take 2–3 apricots, stone them carefully and cut the flesh into thin slices. Set aside for the garnish. Stone the remaining apricots and then purée in a blender or pass through a fine sieve. Mix with the lemon juice, white wine and sugar. Chill until required.

Serve in deep glass bowls garnished with the reserved sliced apricots. Wine biscuits or semi-sweet crisp biscuits make a good accompaniment. SERVES 4

Taramasalata

(Illustrated on page 33)

This is still one of the most popular Greek appetisers. A delicious creamy pâté, it can be used as a spread for canapés, as a dip for raw vegetables or simply in its traditional role as a starter with small wedges of toast.

100 g/4 oz smoked cod's roe, skin removed
4 slices white bread
3 tablespoons lemon juice
200 ml/7 fl oz olive oil
1 small onion, peeled and finely grated
1 teaspoon chopped fresh dill (optional)
GARNISH
black olives (optional)
lemon slices (optional)

Soak the cod's roe in water for 5 minutes to remove some of the salt then drain. Trim and discard the crusts from the bread and soak in about 3 tablespoons of water for 2 minutes, remove and squeeze dry.

Place the cod's roe, bread, lemon juice, oil, onion and dill if used, in a blender and blend until smooth. Alternatively, mash the cod's roe, bread, onion and dill by hand with a fork. When smooth, blend in the lemon juice and olive oil slowly, stirring constantly, until well blended. Beat with a whisk until pink and creamy. Chill before serving garnished with black olives and twists of lemon, if used. SERVES 4–6

Buckling Stuffed Lemons

One of the most elegant ways to start a dinner party
meal is to serve this rich, buttery buckling pâté in their
own lemon cases. The pâté mixture is too thick and dry to
blend so must be done by hand using a pestle and mortar
or wooden spoon.

1 large (200-g/7-oz) buckling
4 lemons
100 g/4 oz unsalted butter
1 garlic clove (optional)
freshly ground black pepper
GARNISH
4 bay leaves

Place the buckling in a small basin and cover with boiling water.
Leave to soak for 1 minute. Drain and cut off the tail. Carefully cut
along the belly and the backbone to remove the skin, open out and
remove the backbone and any other visible bones. Place in a mortar
and pound with a pestle to reduce slightly.

Meanwhile, cut the tops from the lemons and set aside. Cut a small
sliver from the base of each lemon so that they will stand upright.
Scoop the lemon flesh from the lemon cases, reserve, and using a
small teaspoon, squeeze the flesh through a sieve to extract the
lemon juice.

Add the butter to the buckling with the garlic, if used, and pound
until the mixture is reduced to a thick paste. Stir in 1 tablespoon of
the lemon juice and add black pepper to taste. Check the seasoning
and add more lemon juice if liked. Spoon the mixture back into the
lemon shells, replace the lemon caps and chill for 30 minutes.

Just before serving, tuck a bay leaf under the cap of each lemon
and serve the buckling pâtés with freshly made toast. SERVES 4

Kipper Cocktail

(Illustrated on page 33)

Far cheaper and more original than shrimp or prawn
cocktail, this Kipper Cocktail makes a very elegant
appetiser. Serve in small wine or sherry glasses with
brown bread and butter rolls. Make these using thin slices
of buttered, fresh bread with their crusts removed and
roll up tightly like miniature Swiss rolls.

1 (200-g/7-oz) can kipper fillets
1 (142-ml/5-fl oz) carton soured cream
½ lemon
1 tablespoon tomato ketchup
2 teaspoons French mustard
3 tablespoons mayonnaise
salt and freshly ground black pepper
2 large dessert apples
3 celery sticks
50 g/2 oz cashew nuts
GARNISH
parsley sprigs or celery leaves

Drain the canned kippers and cut into small bite-sized pieces.

Turn the soured cream into a mixing bowl and beat until smooth
and creamy. Grate the zest from the half lemon and add to the
soured cream with the tomato ketchup, mustard and mayonnaise.
Stir well to blend then season to taste with salt and freshly ground
black pepper.

Core the apples and cut into small chunks. Put into a bowl with
the kippers and sprinkle with lemon juice squeezed from the half
lemon. Clean and slice the celery and add to the kipper and apple
mixture together with half of the nuts.

Pour the sauce over the kipper and apple mixture and toss lightly
so that the ingredients are lightly coated. Divide the mixture
between six glasses, cover and chill for at least 1 hour.

Serve the cocktails chilled, sprinkled with the remaining nuts and
garnished with parsley sprigs or celery leaves. SERVES 6

Portuguese Pâté

This Portuguese sardine pâté is marvellously quick and
easy to make. The sharp flavours of the mustard, lemon
and onion act as an excellent foil for the richness
of sardines and combine to produce a tasty hors d'oeuvre
at a very reasonable cost. They are especially delicious
if served with fingers of toast sprinkled with chopped
herbs such as parsley or chives.

1 (225-g/8-oz) can sardines in oil
4 teaspoons French mustard
4 teaspoons lemon juice
3 tablespoons curd cheese
salt and freshly ground black pepper
few drops anchovy essence (optional)
1 shallot or pickling onion

Drain the oil from the canned sardines and turn the fish into a
mixing bowl. Mash to a pulp using a fork. Stir the mustard, lemon
juice and curd cheese into the mixture and beat to blend. Season
with salt and freshly ground black pepper and add a few drops of
anchovy essence, if used.

Peel and finely chop the shallot or pickling onion and fold into the
pâté. Pack the pâté into a small terrine before serving. SERVES 6–8

Brandied Turkey Mousse

Turkey blended with eggs, cream, brandy and herbs makes a delicious mousse simple enough to make in a trice and yet impressive enough for a celebration cold table or sumptuous dinner party starter.

1 (70-g/2½-oz) packet aspic jelly powder
600 ml/1 pint turkey or chicken stock, made with 600 ml/1 pint boiling water and a chicken stock cube
225 g/8 oz cooked, boned, smoked turkey, finely diced
1 tablespoon tomato purée
1 teaspoon dried tarragon
2 egg yolks
250 ml/8 fl oz double cream
100 ml/4 fl oz brandy
salt and freshly ground black pepper
lettuce leaves
1 chicory, separated into leaves
GARNISH
orange wedges

Place the aspic in a small bowl. Gradually add the very hot stock, whisking well to dissolve. Leave until cool.

Place all the ingredients except the lettuce leaves and chicory into a blender and blend until smooth and creamy. Turn into a 1.25-litre/2-pint fluted mould and chill until set.

To serve, line a serving plate with the lettuce leaves. Turn the mousse out on to the plate and garnish the outer edge with chicory leaves. Just before serving, garnish with orange wedges and serve with Melba toast. SERVES 4

Asparagus
and Parma Ham Rolls

(Illustrated on front jacket)

Asparagus and Parma Ham Rolls make the perfect appetiser to a dinner party meal or splendid cold food item in a summer or winter buffet.

1 (275-g/10-oz) can asparagus tips
salt and freshly ground black pepper
2 tablespoons mayonnaise
5 thin slices Parma ham
GARNISH
chopped parsley (optional)

Drain the asparagus tips well and cut into 7.5-cm/3-inch lengths. Finely chop the remains of the tips and season well. Fold into the mayonnaise. Sandwich four asparagus tips together using a little of the mixture and roll in a slice of Parma ham, so that the asparagus tips just poke out. Repeat with the remaining slices of ham. Place on a serving dish and garnish with chopped parsley, if used. MAKES 5

Fish and Shellfish

Fish and shellfish exist in such astonishing variety that they can be a perpetual source of delight to the no-cook cook and diner alike. Many no-cook raw and cured fish dishes are already international favourites like Scottish smoked salmon, Scandinavian pickled herrings, German rollmops and fresh oysters. While other raw and smoked delicacies that have won acclaim include Gravad Lax or pickled salmon and Taramasalata or Greek smoked cod's roe pâté.

However, the repertoire shouldn't stop here for there is a whole host of exciting new ways with raw, pickled, smoked and salted fish and shellfish in this chapter. Try Mexican Ceviche – marinated mackerel in lime or lemon juice or Oyster Cocktail just for starters. And since there wasn't room to include it, try deliciously simple Japanese Sashimi – tasty thin strips of raw white fish carefully arranged in Japanese fashion on a plate and served with soy and horseradish sauce.

It goes without saying that the fish you use for raw fish dishes should be superbly fresh. If you are in any doubt about the freshness, use frozen fish as a substitute to fresh since it is frozen on board boat at the peak of perfection.

Ceviche

This Mexican raw fish dish needs at least 4 hours marinating time for the full flavours to develop. Serve with crusty farmhouse bread or warm tortillas for a truly Mexican feast.

2 medium mackerel, cleaned
150 ml/¼ pint lemon juice
2 large tomatoes, peeled and chopped
1 fresh hot chilli pepper, seeds removed and chopped
1 medium onion, peeled and chopped
2 tablespoons chopped parsley
1 teaspoon ground coriander
3 tablespoons olive oil
1 tablespoon vinegar
1 ripe avocado

Open out the fish on a board and press along the backbone to loosen it, then remove. Divide each fish into two fillets, then cut into squares about 1 cm/½ inch in size.

Place the fish in a shallow dish and pour over the lemon juice. Cover and allow to stand in a cool place for at least 4 hours, stirring from time to time.

Mix the tomatoes and chilli with the onion, parsley, coriander, olive oil and vinegar. Drain the fish, reserve the lemon juice and toss with the tomato mixture then arrange in a serving dish.

Peel the avocado, discard the stone then cut the flesh into slices. Brush with a little of the lemon juice discarded from the fish and place on top of the fish mixture. SERVES 4

Gravad Lax

(Illustrated on page 34)

This Swedish delicacy is not an everyday dish, but it is ideal for a celebration meal. It can be served as an appetiser at a dinner party or as part of a cold buffet.

1 (1-kg/2¼-lb) piece middle-cut fresh salmon
60 g/2½ oz castor sugar
¼ teaspoon saltpetre
large bunch fresh dill or 2 tablespoons dried
60 g/2½ oz coarse sea salt
10 peppercorns, crushed
MUSTARD SAUCE
2 tablespoons German mustard
1 egg yolk
1 tablespoon castor sugar
2 tablespoons vinegar
7 tablespoons oil
1 tablespoon chopped fresh dill or dried
salt and freshly ground black pepper
GARNISH
1 lemon, cut into wedges

Scrape and dry the salmon but do not wash. Halve along the backbone and remove this and any other visible bones. Mix the sugar and saltpetre together and rub the fish on all sides with the mixture.

Sprinkle some of the dill on the base of a shallow dish. Place half the salmon on top, skin side down. Sprinkle with more dill, half the sea salt and the crushed peppercorns. Place the other piece of salmon, skin side uppermost, on top and cover with the remaining sea salt and some dill, reserving some for garnish. Cover with a wooden chopping board and weight heavily to press the salmon firmly together.

Keep in a cool, dark place for at least 48 hours. (The dish will keep for 1 week if kept cold.)

Make the mustard sauce for serving by mixing the mustard, egg yolk, sugar and vinegar together. Add the oil slowly, whisking all the time until well blended. Add the chopped dill then season with salt and pepper.

Arrange the salmon on a wooden board or serving dish and garnish with the reserved sprigs of dill, if used and lemon wedges. Carve in fairly thick slices, discarding the skin before serving. Serve with mustard sauce, freshly made toast, lager and cold schnapps, or if you prefer, a chilled white wine. SERVES 6

Marinated Kipper Fillets

It is essential to buy very fresh kippers for this
dish. Ask your fishmonger to fillet them for you, if
possible. The tangy marinade will break down any little
bones that may remain.

8 kipper fillets
1 small onion
3 tablespoons lemon juice
4 tablespoons olive oil
6 black peppercorns
2 bay leaves

Skin the kipper fillets and remove any obvious bones. Lay the fillets
in a flat dish just large enough to hold them.

Peel the onion, slice thinly into rings and place over the top of the
kipper fillets. Mix the lemon juice and oil together and pour over
the kippers. Tuck the peppercorns and bay leaves between the fish
so that they are immersed in the marinade. Cover with clingfilm
and leave to marinate for at least 8 hours or overnight.

Drain the fillets from the marinade before serving. SERVES 4

Raw Sardine Fillets Marinated in Olive Oil and Lime Juice

This is a very popular fish dish around the area of Lyons in France. It is essential to use very fresh sardines; ask your fishmonger to fillet them for you.

16 fresh sardines, filleted
salt and freshly ground black pepper
chervil leaves (optional)
MARINADE
juice of 1 lime
175 ml / 6 fl oz olive oil
salt and freshly ground black pepper
5 coriander seeds
75 g / 3 oz carrots, peeled and cut into julienne strips
75 g / 3 oz fresh fennel, cut into julienne strips

Season the sardine fillets with the salt and pepper and place in a dish.
To make the marinade, blend the lime juice with the olive oil. Season with salt and pepper and add the crushed coriander seeds, carrot strips and fennel strips. Pour over the sardine fillets. Place the dish in the refrigerator and leave to marinate for at least 4 hours, turning the fillets every hour.
To serve, remove the fillets from the marinade and drain. Place on chilled plates and top with the drained, marinated vegetables. Garnish with a few leaves of chervil, if used. SERVES 4

Oyster Cocktail

Oysters in a piquant sauce resting on a bed of lettuce make an elegant start to a dinner party. Serve with small squares of brown bread and butter and a well-chilled white Chablis wine.

2 tablespoons tomato purée
1 teaspoon Worcestershire sauce
1 tablespoon lemon juice
$\frac{1}{4}$ teaspoon salt
$\frac{1}{8}$ teaspoon freshly ground black pepper
150 ml/$\frac{1}{4}$ pint double cream
16 fresh oysters, shelled
1 small crisp lettuce, washed and separated into leaves
GARNISH
1 lemon, sliced
$\frac{1}{2}$ small cucumber, sliced

In a large mixing bowl, combine the tomato purée, Worcestershire sauce, lemon juice, salt and pepper. Add the cream and beat well to combine all the ingredients. Stir in the oysters, coating them thoroughly with the sauce.

Line four individual serving glasses with the lettuce leaves. Spoon equal amounts of the oyster mixture on to the lettuce leaves. Garnish with lemon slices and cucumber twists. Chill for 30 minutes before serving. SERVES 4

Ceviche of Scallops

This is a delightful variation of the Mexican raw fish
dish Ceviche, but uses scallops as the fish ingredient.
Serve with warm crusty bread such as granary.

10 large scallops
150 ml/¼ pint lemon juice
1½ tablespoons finely chopped shallots
½ tablespoon chopped fresh tarragon
½ tablespoon chopped fresh dill
½ tablespoon chopped chives
½ tablespoon chopped fresh parsley
1½ tablespoons oil

Detach the scallops from their shells and scrape off the beard-like
fringe and intestinal thread. Cut away the orange flesh. Wash the
white meat and pat dry. Cut into slices about 5 mm/¼ inch thick.
Wash and prepare the coral in the same way, if you like. Choose 4
medium scallop shells, scrub them well and leave to drain. Put the
scliced scallops in a bowl and pour over the lemon juice. There
should be enough lemon juice to cover the scallop slices. Cover
with clingfilm and chill for 24 hours, stirring occasionally.

When ready to serve, chop the shallots and the herbs very finely
indeed. Drain and discard the lemon juice from the scallops and stir
in the oil. Add the shallots and the herbs and mix well. Spoon on to
the shells and serve immediately with brown bread and butter.
SERVES 4

*Kipper Cocktail (see page 22); Taramasalata (see page 20);
Gazpacho (see page 17)*

Crab Louis with Cucumber

This crab mousse-like mixture is best served with toasted brown bread, wholewheat crackers or Greek brown bread.

300 ml/½ pint Easy Mayonnaise (see page 68)
2 tablespoons tomato ketchup
3 tablespoons olive oil
1 tablespoon wine vinegar
2 tablespoons grated onion
2 tablespoons finely chopped fresh parsley
6 tablespoons double cream, whipped
Tabasco or Worcestershire sauce (optional)
salt and freshly ground black pepper
cayenne pepper
1–2 tablespoons chopped, stuffed olives
450 g/1 lb crabmeat, flaked
thinly sliced peeled cucumber
lettuce leaves
GARNISH
2 tablespoons chopped chives

Blend the first seven ingredients together. Season with Tabasco or Worcestershire sauce, if used, salt, pepper and dash of cayenne to taste.

Stir in the chopped olives and chill for at least 1 hour before serving.

When ready to serve, fold the flaked crabmeat into the sauce. Decorate the outer edge of a serving dish with a ring of overlapping cucumber slices. Lay crisp lettuce leaves in the centre and pile the crabmeat mixture on top. Garnish with chopped chives before serving. SERVES 4–6

Smoked Mackerel Monaco (see page 36); Shrimp and Crabmeat Spread (see page 39); Gravad Lax (see page 28)

Smoked Mackerel Monaco

(Illustrated on page 34)

The richness of smoked mackerel is beautifully contrasted in this dish with a crunchy salad of raw celery, apple and soured cream. This is a rich dish, so portions are naturally small – the ideal light recipe for a working lunch.

450 g/1 lb smoked mackerel
2 crisp dessert apples
1½ tablespoons lemon juice
3 celery sticks
1 (142-ml/5-fl oz) carton soured cream
freshly ground black pepper
2 tablespoons freshly chopped parsley
GARNISH
1 small sweet red pepper

Cut the head and tail from the mackerel. Carefully cut through the skin along the length of the belly and the backbone and remove all the skin. Open the mackerel out flat and remove the backbone and any other visible bones. Using two forks, break up the mackerel flesh into small bite-sized pieces.

Core and cut the apples into small dice. Put into a small basin with the lemon juice and stir until well coated. Wash and chop the celery sticks into small dice and add to the apples. Pour over the well-mixed soured cream, add a sprinkling of freshly ground black pepper and the chopped parsley. Mix well to combine.

Divide the soured cream mixture into roughly four portions and spoon on to four chilled plates. Divide the mackerel into four portions and arrange the mackerel chunks around the soured cream mixture.

Cut the red pepper into thin strips and arrange in a lattice effect across the soured cream mixture before serving. SERVES 4

Smoked Trout with Apple and Horseradish Cream

This is a light supper or lunch dish that comes from
the luxury class. If you wish, the fish can be filleted
and the heads and tails removed beforehand but it is, however,
more usual to serve the fish unfilleted. Serve the sauce
separately in a sauceboat.

4 small smoked trout
1 lettuce heart
4 parsley sprigs
1 lemon, cut into wedges
APPLE AND HORSERADISH CREAM
1 large cooking apple
1 tablespoon lemon juice
1 tablespoon horseradish sauce
3 tablespoons double cream or soured cream

Fillet the fish, if liked, then place on a dish on a bed of lettuce heart.
Cover the fish eyes with the parsley sprigs and garnish with lemon
wedges between each fish.

Wash and quarter the apple, removing the core. Grate the apple,
including the skin on the coarse side of a grater. Immediately, add
the lemon juice to stop the apple flesh from discolouring. Stir in the
horseradish sauce and the cream or soured cream, mixing well.
Spoon into a sauceboat and serve with the smoked trout. SERVES 4

Herring Fillets in Oil

For this dish you will need raw, salted herrings from a barrel. These are becoming more easily available, and can now be found in many delicatessens, especially those specialising in Eastern European food. This is a delicious fish dish, well worth the two days you will have to wait for it. The long marinating in oil with lemon and onion mellows the flavour of the herrings, and gives them a soft, almost buttery texture.

4 salt herrings, washed, filleted, skinned and soaked in water for 24 hours, changing the water occasionally
2 medium Spanish onions, thinly sliced into rings
6 black peppercorns
2 bay leaves, roughly crumbled
1 lemon, thinly sliced
150 ml/$\frac{1}{4}$ pint olive oil

Drain the herring fillets thoroughly, pat them dry with absorbent kitchen paper and lay them in a shallow serving dish. Scatter the onion rings over the herring fillets together with the peppercorns and the crumbled bay leaves. Place the lemon slices on top of the mixture. Pour in the olive oil so that it is just enough to cover the herring fillets. Cover the dish with foil and refrigerate for at least 48 hours before serving. SERVES 4

Shrimp and Crabmeat Spread

(Illustrated on page 34)

Shrimp and Crabmeat Spread makes an excellent starter
if served with triangles of granary toast or a luxury sandwich
filling for picnics or packed lunches.

100 g / 4 oz crabmeat
50 g / 2 oz butter, softened
2 tablespoons double cream
⅛ teaspoon cayenne pepper
¼ teaspoon salt
1 teaspoon lemon juice
225 g / 8 oz shrimps

Place the crabmeat, butter and cream in a mortar and using a pestle,
blend the mixture until smooth. Alternatively, place the ingredients in a liquidiser and blend for about 30 seconds.

Spoon the mixture into a mixing bowl. Add the cayenne, salt and
lemon juice and mash to blend. Finally add the shrimps. Spoon into
a serving bowl and cover. Chill for 1 hour before serving. SERVES 4;
MAKES 350 g / 12 OZ

Meat and Poultry

For centuries, man has eaten his meat cooked, forgetting perhaps that in his early days he ate the same raw. Surprisingly few dishes still exist today where meat is eaten in its raw state – a quick survey would, I'm sure, produce classic Steak Tartare, but then would ponder and search for others. Within this chapter, you will find some of the more unusual ways to serve meat raw that are just as delicious as its cooked meat counterpart. Try Carpaccio, thin slices of beef served with a spicy piquant sauce, for starters.

Not forgetting, of course, the endless variety of cooked, cured, smoked and pickled meats that adorn our delicatessen displays today. There are dishes using salami, Italian Parma ham, French Bayonne and German Westphalia ham. Smoked sausages, turkey and chickens will add yet more variety to meals without running the risk of perhaps cooking the most difficult of foods with the highest cost of possible failure.

Steak Tartare

Originally, true Steak Tartare was made from the meat of a freshly killed young colt which the Huns and Mongols used to put under their saddles to tenderise. With time however, this dish has been adapted and today it is only made with the very best quality raw beef. It has become a classic and addictive French dish.

450 g / 1 lb good quality fillet, rump or sirloin steak, minced
salt and freshly ground black pepper
4 teaspoons chopped parsley
1 tablespoon Worcestershire sauce
juice of 1 lemon
4 egg yolks
2 onions, peeled and chopped
1 large green pepper, seeds removed and chopped
1 large red pepper, seeds removed and chopped
2 tablespoons chopped capers

Place the minced steak in a mixing bowl and gradually work in the seasoning, parsley, Worcestershire sauce and lemon juice. Divide into four portions and shape into flat cakes. Place on four individual serving dishes and make a hollow in the centre of each steak. Place an egg yolk in each hollow, or, if you wish, each yolk can be left in its half shell. Arrange the onions, green pepper, red pepper and capers in neat mounds around the steak tartares.

To serve, mix the onions, peppers and capers into the meat using a knife and fork. Serve at once. SERVES 4

Melon and Ham Gondolas

(Illustrated on page 51)

Sweet, ripe melon combines perfectly with Italian raw smoked ham, known as Prosciutto, or with the Westphalian variety from Germany.

$\frac{1}{2}$ *large ripe Honeydew melon*
6 wafer-thin slices smoked ham
juice of 1 lemon
freshly ground black pepper
GARNISH
lemon wedges
parsley or watercress sprigs

Chill the melon thoroughly. Cut into six long slices, scoop out the seeds and cut the skin away. Place one piece of melon on each slice of ham and wrap the ham neatly over the melon.

Sprinkle with the lemon juice and freshly ground black pepper.

Serve the melon gondolas garnished with wedges of lemon and parsley or watercress sprigs. SERVES 6

Ham and Tongue Mousse

Beaten egg whites are folded through this savoury cold mousse to give it a soufflé texture. It is then poured into a soufflé dish complete with paper collar to set, so that it looks like a hot risen soufflé. Serve as a light lunch dish or dinner party starter.

450 g / 1 lb smoked ham
175 g / 6 oz ox tongue
freshly ground black pepper
15 g / ½ oz powdered gelatine
300 ml / ½ pint double cream
3 egg whites
GARNISH
slices of cucumber

Prepare a 750-ml/1¼-pint soufflé dish by tying a collar of double thickness foil about 5 cm/2 inches deep round the top.

Chop the ham then pound to a purée – an electric blender will do this in seconds. Cut the tongue into small dice and mix the two meats together. Season with freshly ground black pepper.

Dissolve the gelatine in 150 ml/¼ pint hot or boiling water and add to the meat mixture. Whip the cream until lightly thick and fold into the meat mixture. Whisk the egg whites until very stiff and fold through the mixture with a metal spoon. Turn the mixture into the prepared soufflé dish and leave in the refrigerator to set.

To serve, carefully remove the collar and garnish the mousse with thin slices of cucumber. SERVES 6–8

Carpaccio

(Illustrated on page 51)

Carpaccio is a delicious dish of very finely sliced beef
with a spicy sauce. The beef is eaten raw and therefore
a good quality cut of meat should be used so that the meat
is beautifully tender.

450 g / 1 lb lean topside of beef, trimmed of all fat
SPICY SAUCE
6 tablespoons Vinaigrette Dressing (see page 59)
2 anchovies, soaked, filleted, rinsed and dried
1 tablespoon capers
1 tablespoon chopped onion
1 teaspoon Dijon mustard
1 tablespoon chopped gherkins

Chill the meat in the freezer for about 1 hour until it is very cold,
even partially frozen; this facilitates paper-thin slicing. Slice the
meat across the grain into thin transparent strips and arrange the
rolled slices side by side on a serving dish.

Blend all the ingredients for the sauce together in a liquidiser for
just 1 second (the sauce should be grainy) or break down in a food
mill. Serve the meat and the sauce separately. SERVES 4

German Sausage Medley

Sliced frankfurters, German beer sausage or Bratwurst and Gruyère cheese spiced up in a piquant dressing makes a delicious luncheon or supper dish when served with hot bread.

2 frankfurters
1 (225-g/8-oz) Bratwurst sausage
50 g/2 oz Gruyère cheese
DRESSING
2–3 gherkins
3 tablespoons oil
1 tablespoon wine vinegar
½ teaspoon salt
2 teaspoons lemon juice
1 shallot, finely chopped
freshly ground black pepper
½ teaspoon Dijon mustard
1 tablespoon finely chopped fresh parsley

Slice the frankfurters obliquely into thin slices and slice the Bratwurst into matchstick pieces. Cut the cheese into fine strips and combine with the sausages.

To make the dressing, chop the gherkins finely and place in a jar with the other dressing ingredients and shake well to blend. Pour the dressing over the sausages and cheese, toss well and serve at once in a serving dish with hot crusty bread. SERVES 4

Salami and Melon Mayonnaise

A simple meat and fruit dish that is suitable to serve as a
starter or part of a cold buffet. Use lightly oiled kitchen
scissors to cut the shreds of salami, then wash the blades
before snipping the parsley.

1 medium melon
4 slices salami
4 tablespoons thick mayonnaise
1 tablespoon lemon juice
salt and freshly ground black pepper
GARNISH
parsley

Quarter the melon and discard the seeds. Cut the flesh into 1-cm/
½-inch pieces and refrigerate covered. Cut the salami into fine strips
and stir through the mayonnaise with the lemon juice and
seasoning to taste. Cover with clingfilm and refrigerate.

Just before serving, drain the melon and fold through the
mayonnaise and salami mixture. Spoon into individual glasses and
garnish with snipped parsley. Serve with brown bread and butter.
SERVES 6

Salami and Melon Italian Style

This is a delightfully simple dish of slices of salami with slices of melon topped with a spicy dressing. Serve the dressing separately so that everyone can use the amount they like.

1 small Casaba melon
16 paper-thin slices of Italian salami
small bunch of watercress
4 tablespoons olive oil
1½ tablespoons lemon juice
salt and freshly ground black pepper

Chill the ripe melon in the refrigerator for about 1 hour before preparing it. Cut it in half lengthways and cut each half into four long slices. Scoop out the seeds and remove the skin.

Arrange four slices of salami on each plate and set two melon slices on top.

Wash the watercress and trim. Set aside a few sprigs for garnishing the melon and salami and place the rest in a salad sauce-boat.

Make a dressing from the oil and lemon juice by mixing vigorously together. Season to taste and pour over the watercress in the sauce-boat. Garnish the salami and melon with the remaining watercress and serve the sauce or dressing separately. SERVES 4

Tomatoes with Proscuitto

Ideally, one should use Parma ham (Proscuitto) for this recipe but any number of other hams could be used such as Bayonne, Westphalia or Morvan.

4 medium tomatoes
salt and freshly ground black pepper
2 teaspoons chopped fresh basil
100 g / 4 oz raw ham
2 teaspoons chopped capers
1 teaspoon finely chopped onion
4 tablespoons mayonnaise
GARNISH
parsley sprigs

Cut the tops from the tomatoes and scoop out and discard the seeds from their centres using a teaspoon. Sprinkle the insides with salt, pepper and basil.

Chop the raw ham finely and place in the bottom of the tomato shells. Add the capers and onion to the mayonnaise and spoon into the tomatoes on top of the ham. Garnish each tomato with a sprig of parsley and chill before serving with brown bread and butter.

SERVES 4

Wurst Salat

Wurst Salat is the name for a delicious salad made of mixed cooked German wurst or sausages, peppers and onion with gherkins. Serve with rye bread for a hearty main meal.

450 g / 1 lb mixed cooked German wurst, sliced
1 medium green pepper, seeds removed and sliced
1 medium red pepper, seeds removed and sliced
1 onion, peeled and thinly sliced into rings
6 tablespoons Vinaigrette Dressing (see page 59)
2 small pickled gherkins, halved

Arrange the wurst and green and red peppers decoratively on a serving plate. Scatter over the onion rings. Pour over the dressing and garnish with the gherkin halves. Chill for about 30 minutes before serving. SERVES 4

49

Smoked Chicken Pâté

A smooth, creamy pâté, Smoked Chicken Pâté must be made in
a blender but can also be made with smoked turkey
if smoked chicken is not available. Serve with French bread
or toast.

225 g / 8 oz smoked chicken
rind of ½ lemon
juice of 1 lemon
1 tablespoon chopped parsley
salt and freshly ground black pepper
1 (142-ml / 5-fl oz) carton soured cream
50 g / 2 oz butter
GARNISH
watercress sprigs

Cut the smoked chicken into small pieces and place in the blender.
Blend until the chicken is well chopped. Peel the rind thinly from
the lemon and add to the chicken with the lemon juice, parsley,
seasoning and soured cream. Blend for a few seconds and then add
the butter. Blend until the mixture is smooth and creamy. Transfer
the pâté from the blender goblet to six small serving dishes or 1
large dish and cover. Chill before serving garnished with watercress
sprigs. SERVES 6

Carpaccio (see page 44); Melon and Ham Gondolas (see page 42);
Smoked Sausage and Cheese Salad (see page 53)

Smoked Sausage and Cheese Salad

(Illustrated on page 51)

Smoked sausage and Gouda cheese make a delicious salad when combined in a spicy dressing. Serve as a light luncheon dish, a satisfying starter or as part of an expansible feast when entertaining a crowd.

100 g/4 oz onion, peeled and chopped
4 tablespoons chopped fresh parsley
4 tablespoons oil
2 tablespoons wine vinegar
4 teaspoons French mustard
salt and freshly ground black pepper
450 g/1 lb smoked pork sausage, cut into 3-mm/⅛-inch thick slices
350 g/12 oz Gouda cheese, cut into 1-cm/½-inch cubes

Combine the onion, parsley, oil, vinegar, mustard and salt and pepper to taste in a screwtop jar. Shake the ingredients well together to blend thoroughly.

Put the sausage and cheese in a serving bowl and pour over the dressing. Toss well to mix. Cover and leave the flavours to infuse for about 1 hour. Serve lightly chilled with warm French bread.
SERVES 4

Old English Potted Cheese (see page 61); Five-Herb Butter (see page 69)

Smoked Chicken
in Lemon Mayonnaise

Smoked chicken with pineapple in a lemon mayonnaise makes
a super dish for lunch or dinner. Smoked chickens can generally
be found in most good delicatessens.

1 (1.75-kg/4-lb) smoked chicken
1 small fresh pineapple
juice of 1 lemon
300 ml/½ pint Easy Mayonnaise (see page 68)
salt and freshly ground black pepper
25 g/1 oz walnuts, chopped
GARNISH
watercress sprigs

Remove the meat from the chicken. Slice the white breast meat and
cut the dark wing and leg meat into bite-sized pieces.

Slice the pineapple and remove the skin and centre core. Cut three
slices, halve them and reserve for the garnish. Chop the remaining
pineapple into bite-sized pieces.

Stir the lemon juice into the mayonnaise and season to taste. Mix
about 4 tablespoons of the mayonnaise with the dark meat and
arrange on a serving dish. Cover with the chopped pineapple. Lay
the slices of white meat on top and coat with the remaining
mayonnaise. Sprinkle over the chopped walnuts and garnish the
dish with watercress and the reserved halved slices of pineapple.

SERVES 4–6

Turkey Fiesta

Turkey Fiesta is the name for a mild, sweet curried turkey salad dish that is deliciously different. Serve with wholemeal bread for a hearty meal.

4 tablespoons mayonnaise
2 tablespoons soured cream
2 teaspoons concentrated mild curry sauce
1 tablespoon apricot chutney
225 g/8 oz smoked turkey, coarsely chopped
100 g/4 oz frankfurters, sliced
salt and freshly ground black pepper
1 small lettuce, washed and shredded
GARNISH
1 tomato, sliced

Combine the mayonnaise, soured cream, curry sauce and apricot chutney together. Fold in the turkey, frankfurters and season well. Arrange lettuce around a serving dish and pile the turkey and sausage mixture in the centre. Garnish with tomato slices.
SERVES 3–4

Dairy Produce

No one could deny the value of the humble knob of butter, cube of cheese, spoon of yogurt or scoop of cream cheese in the diet – less so the no-cook cook. The value of such foods is highlighted in such recipes as Old English Potted Cheese – a hearty starter or light supper or lunch dish to be served with toast, Five-Herb Butter – a savoury butter that will add a little sophistication to the plainest of roasts or sandwiches or Herb Coated Yogurt Cheese – a delicious home-made cheese using natural yogurt as the simple ingredient.

Simple they may be, but predictable they are not. Ring the changes by introducing new cheeses like Dolcelatte, Ricotta, Gorgonzola, Fetta and Gruyère into the diet instead of the usual Cheddar.

Experiment with yogurt as a flavouring and topping as well as a dessert with fruit and nuts. Even butter will take on a new significance if flavoured with fresh herbs and spices.

Italian Mushroom Salad

It is essential to use fresh Parmesan cheese for this salad and just as essential is the patience required to shave the cheese into paper-thin slices. The result, however, is deliciously rewarding.

225 g/8 oz very fresh white button mushrooms
juice of ½ lemon
100 g/4 oz Parmesan cheese
2 tablespoons olive oil
salt and freshly ground black pepper

Slice the mushrooms very thinly and immediately sprinkle them with the lemon juice. Shave the Parmesan cheese into wafer-thin slices and sprinkle over the mushrooms. Pour over a thin thread of olive oil, season with salt and freshly ground black pepper and serve with crusty bread. SERVES 4

Mixed Cheese with Herbs

Cream and Gruyère cheese mixed together with Parmesan cheese and seasoning and rolled into herb-coated balls make a delicious lunch for the slimmer or special after dinner cheese dish. Serve with warm water biscuits.

175 g/6 oz full-fat soft cheese
25 g/1 oz Gruyère cheese, grated
25 g/1 oz Parmesan cheese, grated
pinch of mustard powder
salt and freshly ground black pepper
pinch of cayenne pepper
4–6 tablespoons chopped burnet, chervils or chives

Mash the soft cheese with a wooden spoon until smooth then beat in the two grated hard cheeses. Add a pinch of mustard powder and salt and pepper to taste. Stir in a pinch of cayenne, then chill for 2 hours until firm.

Form the cheese into about 15 balls and roll each one in the chopped herbs. Serve with warm water biscuits. SERVES 4–6

Avocados Stuffed with Roquefort Cream

This creamy and light yet satisfying dish of avocados
stuffed with a savoury Roquefort cheese cream is ideal for
a light luncheon or supper dish or substantial starter
to a dinner party meal.

2 ripe avocados
1 tablespoon lemon juice
ROQUEFORT CREAM
65 g / 2½ oz Roquefort cheese
65 g / 2½ oz butter, softened
100 g / 4 oz curd cheese, well drained
salt and freshly ground black pepper
paprika
shredded lettuce

Halve the avocados and remove the stones. Scoop out the flesh
carefully from the avocados and dice. Sprinkle with lemon juice
and set aside.

In a bowl, blend together the Roquefort cheese, butter and curd
cheese to make a smooth paste. Season to taste and add a dash of
paprika. Carefully fold in the diced avocado and return to the
empty avocado shells. Chill until required.

Serve the avocados on a bed of shredded lettuce or on individual
serving dishes. SERVES 4–8

Emmenthal Summer Surprise

Tasty strips of Emmenthal cheese, salami and cooked lean
ham with cucumber slices and dressing make the perfect
summer lunch. When fresh dill isn't available,
use dried but add to the dressing rather than the salad
ingredients.

$\frac{1}{2}$ cucumber
275 g/10 oz Emmenthal cheese
100 g/4 oz salami
100 g/4 oz smoked ham
VINAIGRETTE DRESSING
6 tablespoons olive oil
2 tablespoons herb vinegar
1 teaspoon mustard
salt and freshly ground black pepper
pinch of castor sugar
1 teaspoon finely chopped fresh dill or $\frac{1}{2}$ teaspoon dried
GARNISH
bunch of fresh dill

Wash the cucumber and cut into thin slices without peeling. Cut
the cheese, salami and smoked ham into thin strips. Mix with the
cucumber pieces in a serving bowl.

Make the dressing by mixing together the oil, vinegar, mustard,
salt, pepper and sugar until well blended. Pour over the salad and
leave for 30 minutes, tossing from time to time. Check the
seasoning and add the dill, tossing throughout the salad so it is
evenly distributed. Garnish with a bunch of fresh dill. SERVES 4

Tomatoes with Prune Cheese Stuffing

Tomatoes stuffed with a smooth cream cheese and prune mixture makes a delicious first course or light luncheon dish served with granary bread.

4 large tomatoes
225 g/8 oz cream cheese
4 canned and drained or dried and soaked prunes, stoned and chopped
2 spring onions, finely chopped
1 teaspoon finely chopped fresh basil
¼ teaspoon salt
⅛ teaspoon white pepper
2–3 tablespoons milk
8 lettuce leaves
GARNISH
watercress sprigs

With a sharp knife, cut off 1-cm/½-inch lids from the tops of the tomatoes. Scoop out and discard the seeds. Set the shells and lids aside.

Beat the cream cheese with a wooden spoon until soft. Add the prunes, onion, basil, salt and pepper and mix the ingredients thoroughly. Beat in enough milk to make the mixture the consistency of stiffly whipped double cream.

Spoon or pipe the prune cheese mixture back into the tomato shells and replace the lids on a slant.

Arrange the lettuce leaves on four individual serving dishes. Place a stuffed tomato in the centre of each dish and garnish with sprigs of watercress. SERVES 4

Old English Potted Cheese

(Illustrated on page 52)

Potted cheese is an old English dish and almost any variety of cheese may be used from Stilton to Cheddar. If you do not want to use the port or sherry in the recipe, simply double the amount of herbs used.

75 g/3 oz unsalted butter
225 g/8 oz strong-flavoured cheese, such as mature Cheddar, Cheshire,
Stilton or Double Gloucester, finely grated
2 tablespoons port or brown sherry
1 tablespoon chopped chives
pinch of cayenne pepper
GARNISH
4 walnut halves (optional)

Cream the butter until soft then gradually beat in the finely grated cheese. Stir in the port or sherry, chives and cayenne to taste and blend well. Spoon into one large dish or four ramekins and chill for at least 1 hour. Garnish with the walnut halves, if used, before serving with crisp crackers, crispbread or celery sticks. SERVES 4

Grapefruit Stuffed with Cheese Balls

An unusual and nutritious first course for a dinner party,
Grapefruit Stuffed with Cheese Balls may also be served
as a light main meal.

175 g/6 oz Camembert cheese
25 g/1 oz digestive biscuits, crushed
50 g/2 oz walnuts, crushed
4 grapefruit, halved
3 bananas, mashed
3 fresh peaches, peeled, stoned and mashed

Using a sharp knife, cut the rind from the cheese. Mash or pass
through a fine sieve into a small bowl. Stir in the digestive biscuits
and beat the mixture with a wooden spoon until it is smooth and
firm. Working carefully, shape the mixture into small, walnut-
sized balls. Chill for 30 minutes or until firm.

When firm, coat the cheese balls generously with the crushed
walnuts and set aside.

Using a sharp knife, halve the grapefruits, scoop out the flesh and
place in a mixing bowl with the bananas and peaches. Stir to blend
the ingredients together.

Spoon the fruit mixture back into the grapefruit skins and top
with the cheese balls. Chill for 15 minutes before serving.
SERVES 4–8

Cream and Prawn Pâté with Dill

This is one of the simplest pâtés of all to make. Use
a medium-fat soft cheese such as Ricotta and serve with
toasted fingers of brown bread or crispbread.

350 g / 12 oz peeled prawns
175 g / 6 oz medium-fat soft cheese
3 tablespoons soured cream
2 tablespoons lemon juice
salt and freshly ground black pepper
2½ tablespoons chopped fresh dill or 1¼ tablespoons dried
dash of Tabasco sauce
GARNISH
few unpeeled prawns
fresh dill, if available

Using a blender, purée the prawns, the soft cheese, soured cream
and lemon juice together. Add seasoning to taste and blend again.
Add the dill and a dash of Tabasco and blend again to mix the pâté
thoroughly. Pile into a serving dish and chill.
 Just before serving, garnish the pâté with a few unpeeled prawns
and a few sprigs of fresh dill. SERVES 4

Herb Coated Yogurt Cheese

You can make your own soft-type cheese coated with
dried thyme and sesame seeds by simply straining yogurt
in muslin overnight. This cheese will make a delicious
light meal served with salad and rye bread or wholewheat bread.

600 ml / 1 pint natural yogurt
salt and freshly ground black pepper
2 teaspoons olive oil
1 teaspoon dried thyme
1 teaspoon sesame seeds

Line a colander or strainer with muslin and stand it over a bowl. Tip
the yogurt into the muslin and tie it up with string, to form a bag.
Lift it out of the colander and tie the strings to a tap over a sink and
leave to drain overnight.

Next day, tip the curds from the muslin into a bowl and beat until
smooth. Add a little salt and pepper and the olive oil. Form into a
flat, round shape. Pound the dried thyme and sesame seeds together
with a pestle and mortar then tip on to a piece of greaseproof paper.
Lay the cheese in the paper and turn over so that the cheese is
completely coated in the herbs. Chill in the refrigerator before
serving.

Serve with rye bread or wholewheat bread. SERVES 4

Petit Suisse Salads with Chives

Petit Suisse cheese rolled in chopped chives and served with watercress and tomato salad makes a nourishing lunch dish or picnic meal. Pour over the dressing just before serving.

1 bunch watercress
450 g / 1 lb tomatoes
4 Petit Suisse cheeses
4 tablespoons chopped chives
salt and freshly ground black pepper
pinch of castor sugar
½ teaspoon mustard
1 tablespoon white wine vinegar
3 tablespoons olive oil

Wash the watercress and pat dry. Pick off the tender sprigs and lay them around the rims of four individual plates. Skin and slice the tomatoes and lay them in the centre of the watercress.

Unwrap the Petit Suisses and roll each one in the chopped chives. Lay them on top of the tomatoes. Sprinkle with seasoning to taste.

To make the dressing, mix together the sugar, mustard, vinegar and oil and pour over the salads just before serving. SERVES 4

Home-made Kopanisti

In the ancient days, Greeks considered cheese to be an aphrodisiac. Truth or not, no one can deny the beautiful taste of Greek cheeses like Feta, Kasseri and Kopanisti. Sadly, Kopanisti is not available outside of Greece, but here is a recipe for home-made Kopanisti that is worth the waiting. Serve with crisp crackers, in a Greek salad instead of Feta cheese or in delicate puff pastry triangles called Tiropetes.

1 kg/2¼ lb Feta cheese, rinsed and crumbled
350 g/12 oz Danish blue cheese, crumbled
100 g/4 oz softened butter
1 tablespoon oregano
450 g/1 lb cottage cheese, mashed until smooth
1 tablespoon dried thyme
1 tablespoon freshly ground black pepper
2 tablespoons olive oil

Mix all the above ingredients together except the olive oil to make a smooth paste. Place in a large crock or jar and pour the olive oil over the top. To prevent too much mould from forming, place in a cool place and leave for eight weeks without disturbing.

Mix together the cheese including the mould which will have formed on top and place into small covered jars ready for use. Refrigerate until required. Always mix the Kopanisti before serving. MAKES 1.5 kg/3 lbs

Cucumber Mousse with Ham

A special occasion cold table dish, Cucumber Mousse with Ham is very easy to prepare but looks stunning if set in a ring type mould.

½ tablet lemon-flavoured jelly
150 ml/¼ pint boiling water
1 medium cucumber
salt
2 (225-g/8-oz) cartons cottage cheese
150 ml/¼ pint mayonnaise or soured cream
6 tablespoons boiling water
15 g/½ oz powdered gelatine
freshly ground white pepper
lemon juice or wine vinegar
8 slices cooked ham, rolled

Dissolve the jelly in the boiling water and allow to cool slightly. Make a thin layer with some of the cooled jelly on the bottom of a 900-ml/1½-pint ring mould. Thinly slice one quarter of the unpeeled cucumber. Quarter the slices and arrange on the jelly. Allow to set.

Peel the remaining cucumber, cut in half lengthways and remove the seeds. Chop the flesh and place in a colander. Sprinkle with salt and leave for 1 hour to draw out the juices. Rinse and drain well, then pat dry with absorbent kitchen paper.

Press the cottage cheese through a fine sieve into a mixing bowl. Stir in the mayonnaise or soured cream.

Place the boiling water in a small bowl, sprinkle over the gelatine and whisk well to dissolve. Stir into the cottage cheese mixture with the remaining jelly. Add salt, pepper and lemon juice or wine vinegar to taste. Finally fold in the chopped cucumber. When the mixture begins to set slightly, pour into the ring mould on top of the jelly mixture. Chill until set.

To turn out the mousse, dip the mould into hot water for 15 seconds, then invert quickly on to a serving dish. Fill the centre of the ring mould with the rolled slices of ham. SERVES 4–6

Easy Mayonnaise

Creamy mayonnaise can literally transform a salad from plain
greenery to exotic fare and nothing tastes better than home-made
mayonnaise. This really is a no-fail recipe whether you make
it by hand or in a blender.

1 egg
1 tablespoon vinegar or lemon juice
½ teaspoon salt
1 teaspoon castor sugar
pinch of mustard powder
pinch of freshly ground white pepper
300 ml/½ pint olive oil or salad oil

Put the whole egg, vinegar or lemon juice and seasonings in a bowl
and work together with a spoon to make a paste. Slowly beat in the
oil, drop by drop, until the mayonnaise is thick. Alternatively,
place the paste in a blender and add the oil slowly with the blender
running on a low speed. MAKES 300 ml/½ pint

Green Goddess Dressing

This delightful herb mayonnaise dressing makes a delicious
addition to mixed salads, or it can be served as a scrumptiously
different filling for jacket potatoes.

250 ml/8 fl oz mayonnaise
1 teaspoon anchovy essence
3 spring onions, finely chopped
2 tablespoons chopped parsley
2 teaspoons chopped tarragon
1 tablespoon tarragon vinegar
½ teaspoon freshly ground black pepper
1 (142-ml/5-fl oz) carton soured cream

In a medium mixing bowl, combine all the ingredients except the
soured cream, and beat well until they are thoroughly blended.
Using a metal spoon, quickly fold in the soured cream. Store in the
refrigerator until required. Serve with salads, crudités or jacket
potatoes. MAKES 450 ml/¾ pint

Five-Herb Butter

(Illustrated on page 52)

It really is so easy to make savoury butters and they certainly do cheer up plain roast meats, boiled vegetables and sandwich fillings. Make this herb butter and store in the refrigerator until needed – it will transform any plain dish into something special.

1 teaspoon chopped fresh parsley
½ teaspoon chopped fresh mint
½ teaspoon chopped fresh chives
½ teaspoon chopped fresh tarragon
½ teaspoon chopped fresh marjoram
1 tablespoon lemon juice
100 g/4 oz butter

Chop the herbs very finely by hand or in a blender and mix with the lemon juice. Cream the butter until light and soft and work in the herb and lemon mixture. Leave to stand at room temperature for 2 hours to allow the flavours to develop, then pack into a screwtop jar and store in the refrigerator until needed. Alternatively, form the lightly chilled butter into a roll, wrap in greaseproof paper and chill then slice before using.

MAKES 100 g/4 oz

Vegetables and Salads

Of all foods, vegetables and salads constitute the most varied and abundant source of nourishment. From the mundane cabbage to the most exotic asparagus, they are a constant inspiration and challenge to the cook. The range and diversity of vegetables and salads prepared without cooking is immense and destined to make any reciter of 'rabbit food' eat their words after sampling such delights as Basil Courgette Salad and Stuffed Pepper Salad.

Perhaps the secret is to follow the seasons, for each new month unlocks a new type of vegetable. Tomatoes, for example, attain their finest flavour in high summer and celery reaches its best flavour deep into winter. The price in shops will help tell you when vegetables are in season.

By using vegetables in season to produce tasty salads and imaginative meals, your diet is bound to taste better and undoubtedly be better for you nutritionally – nature will ensure that it has the virtue of variety.

Basil Courgette Salad

(Illustrated on page 77)

This side dish of grated courgettes in a spicy piquant
dressing should be prepared at the last possible moment.
If fresh basil is not available, substitute fresh tarragon.

5 young courgettes, topped and tailed
12 fresh basil leaves, finely chopped
DIJON DRESSING
4 tablespoons olive oil
2 tablespoons wine vinegar
salt and freshly ground black pepper
1 teaspoon Dijon mustard

Coarsely grate the courgettes into a mixing bowl. Add two-thirds
of the basil and mix well to blend. In a screwtopped jar, add the
remaining basil and all the dressing ingredients. Shake together
until well blended. Pour over the courgettes and toss to coat
thoroughly in the dressing. Serve at once. SERVES 4

Celeriac Rémoulade

Celeriac Rémoulade is splendid when served as an appetiser to a
heavy main course meal or perfect as part of an hors d'oeuvres.

1 medium celeriac
1 tablespoon lemon juice
2 egg yolks
1 tablespoon tarragon vinegar
2 tablespoons French mustard
salt and freshly ground black pepper
2–3 tablespoons olive oil
2–3 tablespoons whipping cream
4 teaspoons chopped parsley and chives

Peel the celeriac root and cut into thin slices, then cut the slices into
long matchstick pieces. Sprinkle with lemon juice. Mix together
the egg yolks, vinegar, mustard, salt and pepper, and gradually
work in the oil and cream.
   Fold the celeriac pieces into the cream sauce and serve sprinkled
with chopped parsley and chives. SERVES 4

Dressed Chicory Spears

Although expensive during the winter months, chicory is cheap and plentiful during the summer and makes an ideal light starter to a special dinner party menu. Dressed Chicory Spears can be made well ahead if the chicory is dipped in lemon juice.

450 g / 1 lb chicory spears
juice of 1 large lemon
1 egg yolk
salt and freshly ground white pepper
150 ml / $\frac{1}{4}$ pint oil
1 red pepper, seeds removed and chopped
1 green pepper, seeds removed and chopped

Cut the base off each head of chicory. Separate the leaves under cold running water and drain thoroughly. Toss in 3 tablespoons of lemon juice and reserve.

Beat the egg yolk with a pinch of salt and some white pepper to taste. Add the oil, a little at a time, whisking continually. When thick, stir in the lemon juice drained from the chicory. Adjust the thickness to a stiff pouring consistency by adding a litter warm water.

Divide the chicory between six large goblets or balloon glasses. Just before serving, spoon over the dressing and sprinkle with the chopped red and green peppers. SERVES 6

Onion Sambal

Onion Sambal is a delicious mixture of onions, yogurt and spices. It is usually served as an accompaniment to curry or other spiced dishes but it is equally good served as part of a cold buffet with cold meats, poultry and fish.

2 medium onions
1 clove garlic
1 tablespoon chopped mint
150 ml/¼ pint natural yogurt
1 teaspoon chilli paste
few drops of Tabasco sauce
salt and freshly ground black pepper
1 teaspoon castor sugar

Peel the onions and slice them thinly into a bowl. Crush the garlic and mix with the remaining ingredients. Spoon over the onion slices and mix well. Serve as soon as possible in a large bowl or individual serving dishes. SERVES 4

Artichoke Bean Bowl

It is extremely useful to have stashed away in your storecupboard a few cans of vegetables and beans to make a simple instant meal, as this recipe shows.

2 tablespoons Vinaigrette Dressing (see page 59)
1 clove garlic, crushed
1 (283-g/10-oz) can red kidney beans, drained
1 onion, peeled and finely sliced
2 large tomatoes, chopped
1 (425-g/15-oz) can artichoke hearts, drained
salt and freshly ground black pepper

Combine the dressing and the garlic in a small bowl. In another larger bowl, combine the beans, onion, tomatoes, artichoke hearts and seasoning to taste. Pour in the dressing and toss well to mix. Chill before serving with crusty French bread. SERVES 4

Danish Cucumber Salad

Cucumber salad is served all over Scandinavia, particularly in the summer, which is probably why in Denmark, the Silly season is called *Agurketid* – cucumber time. Cucumber salad prepared this way will not give you indigestion and is delicious served with most meat dishes and hot or cold salmon.

1 medium cucumber
1 teaspoon salt
6 tablespoons vinegar
100 g / 4 oz castor sugar
6 tablespoons water
freshly ground white or black pepper
3 tablespoons chopped chives

Wash the cucumber and peel if the skin is very tough. Slice thinly into a large bowl and sprinkle with the salt. Toss to spread the salt evenly and leave for about 15 minutes.

Meanwhile, to make the dressing, mix the vinegar, sugar and water together and season with a little pepper.

Squeeze the cucumber to remove as much liquid as possible. Place in a serving bowl and pour over the dressing. Leave to marinate for at least 30 minutes before serving sprinkled with the chives.

SERVES 4

74

Beetroot Salad with Yogurt

An any season salad that can be prepared in no time
at all. Serve with cold cooked or smoked pieces of meat
or fish with warm crusty bread for a satisfying and
memorable meal.

275 g/10 oz small, young, raw beetroot, peeled and finely sliced
2 apples, peeled, cored and thinly sliced
250 ml/8 fl oz natural yogurt
salt and freshly ground black pepper
½ teaspoon castor sugar
juice of 1 lemon
3 tablespoons lemon mayonnaise
1 small onion, finely chopped
2 teaspoons grated fresh horseradish

Mix the beetroot and apple together in a small bowl. Season the
natural yogurt with the salt and freshly ground black pepper, sugar
and lemon juice. Beat in the mayonnaise and mix with the beetroot
and apple. Sprinkle the salad with the chopped onion and grated
fresh horseradish. SERVES 4

Coleslaw Appetiser

Everyone has their favourite recipe for coleslaw and this
is mine – a perfect combination of white cabbage, celery,
carrots, onions, walnuts, raisins and a deliciously flavoured
mayonnaise.

225 g/8 oz white cabbage, cored and finely shredded
75 g/3 oz celery, trimmed and finely chopped
75 g/3 oz carrots, peeled and finely grated
75 g/3 oz onion, peeled and finely chopped
75 g/3 oz walnuts, roughly chopped
75 g/3 oz seedless raisins
grated rind and juice of 1 small lemon
150 ml/¼ pint mayonnaise
2 tablespoons oil
1 tablespoon wine vinegar
1 teaspoon dry mustard
salt and freshly ground black pepper
GARNISH
paprika

Put the cabbage, celery, carrot, onion, walnuts and raisins in a
serving bowl. Combine the lemon rind and juice with the
mayonnaise, oil, vinegar and mustard in a small bowl and add
seasoning to taste. Fold the mayonnaise through the vegetable and
fruit mixture, blending well.
  Serve the coleslaw in individual bowls garnished with a dusting of
paprika. Serve with savoury crackers and pretzels. SERVES 4–6

Stuffed Pepper Salad (see page 80); Basil Courgette Salad (see page 71);
Greek Salad (see page 79)

76

Greek Salad

(Illustrated on page 77)

The Greek philosopher Aristoxenus is said to have loved
lettuce so much that he watered his lettuce garden with the
sweet wine from Chios – perhaps that is why the salad of
the Greeks predominantly features lettuce of all kinds
from Iceberg, Cos and Endive to salad greens such as Romaine,
Chicory and Escarole. When the more unusual varieties of
lettuce are available, use them instead of the Cos lettuce
in the recipe below.

1 Cos lettuce, washed and separated into leaves
1 bunch radishes, sliced
225 g / 8 oz Feta cheese, cubed
½ teaspoon dried marjoram
4 tomatoes, skinned and sliced
6 anchovy fillets, finely chopped
6 large black olives, halved and stoned
1 tablespoon finely chopped fresh parsley
½ teaspoon freshly ground black pepper
DRESSING
4 tablespoons olive oil
4 teaspoons white wine vinegar
1 tablespoon finely chopped mixed fresh herbs
4 spring onions, finely chopped
1 teaspoon castor sugar
pinch of salt
½ teaspoon freshly ground black pepper

Arrange the lettuce on a large dish. Scatter the radish slices over the
lettuce. Pile the cheese in the centre of the dish and sprinkle with the
marjoram. Place the tomatoes in a circle around the cheese and top
with the anchovies and olives. Sprinkle the salad with the parsley
and pepper.

Mix together the dressing ingredients in a screw-topped jar. Shake
to combine and pour over the salad to serve. SERVES 4

Cretan Grapes (see page 91); Mango Prawns (see page 94)

Stuffed Pepper Salad

(Illustrated on page 77)

Peppers are doubly delicious if stuffed with a creamy
mixture of cottage cheese, cream cheese, onion and herbs.
Chilled then sliced, they make a colourful addition to a
cold buffet party spread or delicious lunch-time treat.

2 medium red peppers
2 medium green peppers
175 g/6 oz cottage cheese
350 g/12 oz cream cheese
2 tablespoons chopped chives
1 small onion, peeled and finely chopped
salt and freshly ground black pepper
1 tablespoon freshly chopped parsley
GARNISH
watercress sprigs

Cut away a thin slice of pepper from the stalk end of the peppers
and discard. Remove the seeds and wash the shells thoroughly.

Beat together the cottage cheese, cream cheese, chives, onion,
seasoning to taste and parsley. Stuff the peppers with the seasoned
cheese mixture, pressing down firmly. Chill for at least 1 hour.

To serve, slice the peppers and arrange red and green pepper slices
alternately on a serving dish. Garnish with watercress sprigs.
SERVES 4

Herby Mushroom Salad

Raw mushrooms make a most delicious low-calorie salad when sliced very thinly and mixed with onion, garlic, oil, vinegar, lemon juice and chopped fresh herbs. Serve with cold meats and poultry or as part of a cold buffet.

225 g/8 oz button mushrooms
salt and freshly ground black pepper
2 tablespoons finely chopped onion
1 clove garlic, crushed
4 tablespoons olive oil
1 tablespoon white wine vinegar
½ tablespoon lemon juice
2 tablespoons chopped chervil
2 tablespoons chopped chives

Wipe the mushrooms with a damp cloth; remove and discard their stalks and cut the caps into thin slices. Put them in a serving bowl and add lots of salt and freshly ground black pepper. Stir in the chopped onion and crushed garlic, mixing well. Stir in the oil and wine vinegar and finally the lemon juice and chopped herbs. Serve as soon as possible. SERVES 4

Turkish Pepper Salad

Turkish Pepper Salad is a crispy and fruity combination of
green peppers, raisins, spring onions, pine nuts and piquant
dressing. It is ideal to serve with a casserole dish or
with shish kebabs.

2 medium green peppers
2 tablespoons seedless raisins
2 spring onions, finely chopped
25 g / 1 oz pine nuts
5 tablespoons olive oil
3 tablespoons lemon juice
pinch of paprika
salt and freshly ground black pepper

Remove the seeds and membranes from the peppers and cut the
flesh into thin strips. Soak the raisins in a little warm water for about
15 minutes so that they become plump. Drain well. Mix together
the green pepper, raisins, spring onion and pine nuts and place in a
serving bowl.

Mix the oil, lemon juice, paprika and seasoning together and pour
over the salad mixture. Toss well to mix. SERVES 4

Chinese White Turnip Salad

In the East, the turnip is much appreciated as a raw vegetable thinly sliced and served in a soy-flavoured sauce. Serve with cold meats, cheese and fish.

450 g / 1 lb small young white turnips
1 tablespoon sesame oil
1 teaspoon castor sugar
pinch of ground ginger
1 tablespoon soy sauce
1 tablespoon cider vinegar

Peel the turnips and cut into paper-thin slices. Place in a serving bowl.

Mix the oil, sugar, ginger, soy sauce and vinegar together and pour over the turnips. Toss to coat then leave for 4 hours before serving. SERVES 4

Pear Waldorf Salad

Waldorf Salad originated in the Waldorf Hotel in New York. This is a delicious variation of the original dish and makes a meal in itself.

1 lettuce, washed and shredded
2 sticks celery, diced
1 red pepper, seeds removed and sliced
25 g / 1 oz walnuts
6 green grapes, peeled, halved and seeds removed
1 pear, peeled, cored and sliced
175 g / 6 oz smoked chicken, diced
4 tablespoons mayonnaise
GARNISH
1 pear, halved and cored

Mix all the salad ingredients together in a large bowl and turn into a serving dish. Garnish with the unpeeled pear halves. Chill lightly before serving. SERVES 4

Blue Cheese Lettuce Wedges

In this recipe, wedges of tightly packed lettuce are coated in
a blue cheese dressing. Choose a firm lettuce like a Webb,
Cos or Romaine as the salad ingredient and Roquefort, Danish
blue or Gorgonzola as the cheese.

1 firm lettuce
50 g / 2 oz blue cheese
6 tablespoons mayonnaise
6 tablespoons single cream
salt and freshly ground black pepper
lemon juice to taste
paprika to taste

Trim the lettuce core at the base but do not remove completely.
Wash the lettuce well, drain and cut into six wedges. Place in a
covered container and chill to crisp in the refrigerator before
serving.

Mash the cheese with a fork and gradually add the mayonnaise.
Stir in the cream, beating the mixture well. Season with salt,
pepper, and lemon juice to taste. Pour the dressing over the lettuce
wedges just before serving and sprinkle with a little paprika.
SERVES 6

Panama Radish Salad

Another salad that is delicious when served as an accompaniment to cold meats and fish. Use the large radishes that are often found during the summer months for this dish.

2 tablespoons olive oil
2 tablespoons lemon juice
1½ teaspoons salt
¼ teaspoon freshly ground black pepper
3 large bunches radishes
1 small onion, peeled and sliced
2 medium tomatoes, peeled and chopped
1 teaspoon finely chopped fresh mint
1 lettuce, washed and shredded

To make the dressing, mix together the olive oil, lemon juice, salt and pepper. Wash and trim the radishes then slice into a bowl. Add the sliced onion, tomatoes, and finally the mint. Pour over the dressing and toss to mix well. Chill and serve on a bed of shredded lettuce. SERVES 4–6

Fruit

Fresh fruit makes delicious eating on its own, in fruit salads, meat dishes, with cheese and especially with nuts. The variety of fruits available is as wide as that of vegetables, so while not forgetting the everyday apple, orange, banana and lemon, experiment with the more exotic seasonal fruits such as avocados, melons, pawpaws, kiwi fruit and figs.

Mango Prawns, a delicious concoction of spicy prawns mixed with cubed mango and returned to the mango shell or Fresh Fig and Mint Majesty – ripe pink figs in a creamy mint dressing should inspire even the most jaded palate.

Think of fruit in wider terms – it is not just for eating as a dessert but will liven up a sparse salad during the often barren winter months, will add flavour to lunchtime cheese dishes and can claim many main course dishes in its own right.

Fresh Fig and Mint Majesty

A dish fit to serve a king! Probably best made
during the summer months when fresh figs arrive in our shops
and when fresh mint is in abundant supply.

1 kg/2 lb fresh figs
3 thin slices Prosciutto ham, fat removed
12 fresh mint leaves
juice of 1 lemon
salt
150 ml/¼ pint double cream

Peel the figs and cut each one half way round from the stem end, making two incisions in the form of a cross. Press gently from the sides to open the incisions slightly (as one does with a jacket potato). Arrange the figs close together on a serving dish and chill for about 1 hour in the refrigerator.

Cut the ham into thin julienne strips and set aside. Crush about half of the mint leaves in the lemon juice and leave to marinate for about 20 minutes, then discard the mint. Stir a pinch of salt into the lemon juice and gradually stir in the cream. The acid of the lemon juice will slowly thicken the cream. Taste and adjust the seasoning if necessary.

Sprinkle the figs with half of the ham strips and spoon over the cream dressing. Scatter over the remaining ham and garnish with the remaining mint leaves. SERVES 5–6

Fresh Figs with Yogurt

French or Italian purple-skinned figs with sweet red centres are generally available during the late summer months. This refreshing dessert may well evoke memories of the Mediterranean where it is often found, with fig leaves or vine leaves arranged beneath the dessert glasses in which they are served.

8 fresh figs
150 ml/¼ pint double cream
150 ml/¼ pint natural yogurt
4 tablespoons soft brown sugar

Put the figs in a large bowl of hot water for 1 minute. Drain them thoroughly, peel off the skins and quarter each fig. Whip the cream lightly and blend in the yogurt.

Spoon a little of the cream and yogurt mixture into the bottom of four small dessert glasses. Top with a layer of figs and a layer of brown sugar, followed by more cream mixture, figs, sugar and finishing with a layer of cream.

Chill in the refrigerator for at least 2 hours to allow the sugar to melt into the cream and yogurt mixture. SERVES 4

Melon Boats

Serve these luscious Melon Boats as a first course or as a dessert. Any Musk melon, such as Cantaloupe, Charentais, Honeydew or Ogen melon, may be used.

2 small Musk melons
2 pears, peeled, cored and chopped
100 g/4 oz black grapes, halved and seeds removed
2 teaspoons lemon juice
3 tablespoons clear honey
GARNISH
mint sprigs

Cut the melons in half and, using a spoon, remove the seeds. Using a round melon baller, scoop out the melon flesh into balls.

Transfer the melon balls to a mixing bowl. Add the chopped pears and halved grapes. Stir in the lemon juice and honey, mixing well.

With a sharp-edged spoon, scoop out any flesh remaining in the melon shells and scallop the edges of the shells with a knife, if liked.

Pile the fruit mixture back into the melon boats and chill for 20 minutes. Just before serving, garnish each boat with a sprig of mint.

SERVES 4

Coupe Jacques

A classic French dessert, Coupe Jacques is made of lemon
and raspberry sorbet, served in individual shallow glass bowls,
and moulded so that each half of the bowl is a different
colour. The sorbet is topped with fresh fruit, steeped in
Kirsch and decorated with blanched almonds. Any fruits suitable
for fruit salad may be used.

600 ml/1 pint assorted fresh fruit, cut into small pieces
2 tablespoons castor sugar
2 teaspoons lemon juice
7 tablespoons Kirsch
600 ml/1 pint raspberry sorbet
600 ml/1 pint lemon sorbet
50 g/2 oz blanched almonds, halved

Combine the fruit, sugar, lemon juice and 6 tablespoons of the
Kirsch together in a mixing bowl. Toss and mix well to blend.
Chill for 1 hour.

Put a large tablespoon of raspberry sorbet and another of lemon
sorbet side by side in each of six serving dishes, leaving a small space
between the two sorbets.

Put a large tablespoon of fruit on top and in between the sorbets.
Sprinkle the Coupe Jacques with the remaining Kirsch and top
with the chopped almonds. Serve immediately. SERVES 6

Cretan Grapes

(Illustrated on page 78)

When grapes are in season, the people of Crete often serve them in this unusual fashion. Serve with slices of Kasseri cheese as a snack or on their own as a dessert. If you do not want to use wine or liqueur, dip each cluster of grapes into slightly beaten egg white instead.

1 kg / 2¼ lb seedless grapes
175 ml / 6 fl oz Mavrodaphne wine, Ouzo or Crème de Menthe
175 g / 6 oz icing sugar, sifted

Wash the grapes thoroughly and drain. Cut the stems to make small clusters of grapes. Dip each cluster of grapes into the wine or liqueur and dust generously with icing sugar. Place on a baking sheet and put in the freezer or ice-making compartment of a refrigerator for 30 minutes, then refrigerate until ready to serve. SERVES 6

Stuffed Peaches

It is essential to use ripe peaches for this dish. Serve with crisp crackers or hot toast.

4 ripe peaches
lemon juice
100 g / 4 oz Mycella or other mild blue cheese
2–4 tablespoons cream
GARNISH
lettuce leaves
walnut halves

Chill the peaches in the refrigerator for about 1 hour before preparation. Wipe the peaches clean, cut them in half, remove the stones and enlarge the cavities slightly with a teaspoon. Sprinkle the cut surfaces with lemon juice to prevent them discolouring.
  Stir the cheese with the cream until well mixed and smooth and pile this mixture into the halved peaches. Arrange a bed of lettuce on individual plates and top with the stuffed peaches. Garnish with the halved walnuts. SERVES 4

Pears with Mustard Cream Mayonnaise

A delicious dish to serve as a starter or as a light main meal. Choose perfectly ripe pears that are blemish free for best results and chill slightly before serving.

2 ripe eating pears
1 tablespoon lemon juice
4 tablespoons mayonnaise
1 tablespoon Dijon mustard
2 tablespoons double cream, whipped
GARNISH
lettuce leaves
blanched almonds

Peel the pears, keeping them in a good shape, then using a teaspoon, scoop out the seeds and core. Brush each pear with the lemon juice to prevent them from discolouring.

Whisk the mayonnaise with the mustard and whipped double cream, adding 1 teaspoon of boiling water if the consistency is too thick to coat the pears smoothly.

To serve, place a few lettuce leaves on four small plates. Place a pear half, cut side down, on each plate and coat with the mustard mayonnaise. Split the almonds and toast under the grill until golden brown. Cool and use to garnish the pears. Chill before serving. SERVES 4

Grapefruit and Chicory Salad

This slightly sharp salad goes well with rich meats, such as game or roast pork. Alternatively, serve it on its own with cheese.

2 heads of chicory
2 grapefruit
8 tablespoons olive oil
2 tablespoons white wine vinegar
salt and freshly ground black pepper
Tabasco sauce

Remove any damaged leaves from the chicory. Trim the root ends and scoop out any cores. Wash and dry thoroughly. Cut the chicory crossways, into thin slices and put in a salad bowl.

Squeeze and reserve the juice from half a grapefruit. Peel off the skin from the remaining grapefruit and remove all the white pith. Divide them into segments and cut each segment in half. Mix with the chicory.

Make the dressing by combining the oil, vinegar and reserved grapefruit juice and season to taste with salt and pepper and a few drops of Tabasco. Pour over the salad and toss well. SERVES 4

Mango Prawns

(Illustrated on page 78)

This recipe may be used with crab instead of prawns but still use equal quantities of mango and shellfish.

4 mangoes
8 large Mediterranean type prawns, peeled
1 red pepper, seeds removed and cut into strips (optional)
few fresh mint leaves (optional)
8 whole Mediterranean type prawns to garnish
DRESSING
300 ml/½ pint Easy Mayonnaise (see page 68)
2 tablespoons freshly grated horseradish
1 teaspoon lemon or lime juice
1 teaspoon castor sugar
freshly ground black pepper

Slit the mangoes in half lengthwise all the way round the flesh and in as far as the stone. Remove the peel from one half and cut the flesh off the stone. Carefully cut the stone out of the remaining half and remove the flesh, reserving the skin. Cut the flesh in cubes or balls. Cut the prawns into bite-size chunks and combine with the mango flesh.

Make the dressing by mixing the mayonnaise, horseradish, lemon or lime juice, sugar and black pepper together. Mix the prawns and mango with the dressing and pile into the four reserved mango skins. Garnish with strips of red pepper and mint leaves, if used, and the prawns. Serve chilled. SERVES 4

Khoshaf (see page 114); Cassata Alla Siciliana (see page 113); Raspberry Meringue Gâteau (see page 110)

Lunchtime Avocado

As the name suggests, this is a suitable dish to serve at lunch
or for a light meal during the evening. Do not allow the
avocado to stand for very long before serving or the flesh may
discolour.

2 avocados
4 tablespoons oil
2 tablespoons vinegar
salt and freshly ground black pepper
pinch of dry mustard
175 g/6 oz Cheddar cheese, grated
GARNISH
4 gherkins
2 tomatoes, sliced

Cut the avocados in half lengthwise. Remove the stones and
discard. To make the dressing, place the oil, vinegar, salt, pepper
and mustard into a screwtop jar and shake to mix well.
Place the cheese in a bowl, add the salad dressing, mix thoroughly
then spoon on top of the avocados.
Place the avocados in a shallow serving dish and garnish each with
a gherkin fan and sliced tomatoes. SERVES 4

Hazelnut Truffles (see page 125); Nut and Sultana Bars (see page 124);
Walnut Pairs (see page 119)

Chilled Tomato Emincée

Chilled Tomato Emincée is a deliciously simple concoction
of tomatoes and onions topped with a curry-flavoured
mayonnaise. Served in soup bowls, it makes a light starter
or lunch dish.

10 ripe tomatoes, skinned
1 small onion, peeled
salt and freshly ground black pepper
6 tablespoons mayonnaise
2 tablespoons whipped cream
1½ tablespoons chopped parsley
2 teaspoons curry powder

Halve the skinned tomatoes and remove and discard their seeds.
Finely chop and place in a mixing bowl. Finely grate the onion and
add to the tomatoes. Season well and mix to blend.

Fold the mayonnaise and cream together until well blended. Add
the chopped parsley and curry powder, mixing well.

Spoon the tomato and onion mixture into four individual soup
bowls. Top with a generous dollop of the curry mayonnaise and
chill for at least 30 minutes before serving. SERVES 4

Turnip and Date Salad

A really unusual combination of flavours makes Turnip
and Date Salad an ideal accompaniment to cold roast poultry
such as chicken or duck.

2 tart eating apples, peeled, cored and diced
2 teaspoons lemon juice
1 medium turnip, peeled and finely grated
14 fresh or dried dates, stoned and coarsely chopped
2 teaspoons castor sugar
3 tablespoons single cream
1 small carrot, peeled and finely grated

Place the apples in a salad bowl and sprinkle over the lemon juice.
Add the grated turnip and the chopped dates and sprinkle over 1½
teaspoons of the sugar. Stir carefully with a wooden spoon to
thoroughly combine the ingredients.

 Pour in the cream and, using two large spoons, toss the salad until
the ingredients are well coated. Sprinkle over the grated carrot
mixed with the remaining sugar. Serve immediately. SERVES 4

Home-made Muesli

Muesli, a healthy mixture of whole cereal grains, fruit
and nuts, was originally a Swiss peasant dish, but it became
world famous after it had been adapted as part of a health
diet at the Bircher–Benner Clinic in Switzerland. It is well
worth making your own, not only is it cheaper than brand-name
variations but you can make it as sweet, fruity, nutty
or filling as you like.

225 g/8 oz wholewheat flakes
225 g/8 oz rye flakes
225 g/8 oz whole oat flakes
225 g/8 oz barley flakes
350 g/12 oz mixed roasted nuts
450 g/1 lb mixed dried fruit such as sultanas, apples, prunes, apricots,
figs, dates, chopped
225 g/8 oz seedless raisins

Mix all the ingredients together and store in a dry, cool place before
serving with milk, yogurt or cream. MAKES 2 kg/4¼ lb

Natural Health Squares

Everyone enjoys something a little sweet from time to time,
whether it be an after dinner chocolate or between meal treat –
this recipe fits the bill and is somewhat more healthy.

225 g/8 oz dates, stoned
450 g/1 lb dried figs
275 g/10 oz walnuts, chopped
50 g/2 oz seedless raisins
450 g/1 lb dried apricots
1 teaspoon grated orange rind, sesame seeds, or shredded unsweetened
coconut

Put all the ingredients except the orange rind, sesame seeds or
coconut in a blender and mix well. Press into two 18-cm/7-inch
square shallow, buttered trays. Cut into 2.5-cm/1-inch squares.
Roll in the orange rind, sesame seeds or coconut. MAKES 49 pieces

Puddings and Desserts

When all good food affords pleasure, it is desserts that are devised for pleasure alone. Such is the weight and importance laid on the shoulders of the dish that ends the meal with grace and favour. The no-cooks repertoire of puddings and desserts is a formidable one containing dishes as widely different as Khoshaf, a dried fruit salad scented with rose water to light-as-a-feather Raspberry Meringue Gâteau made with no-cook meringue.

So whether you want a simple dessert to finish a mid-week family meal like Orange Posset or a grand dinner party centre-piece like Sicilian Cassata, you'll find lots of ideas here.

Not just designed for summer time eating, these puddings and desserts will prove invaluable for winter time entertaining when a no-cook cook-ahead dessert is the order of the day.

Chestnut and Orange Whirls

The perfect instant dessert to serve when unexpected guests
arrive. Whisked up in no time at all, this recipe combines
the nutty flavour of chestnuts with the sharp tangy flavour
of oranges. Very pretty too when piped into tall glasses
and topped with chopped mixed nuts.

1 (440-g/15½-oz) can sweetened chestnut purée
1 large orange
50 g/2 oz icing sugar, sifted
2 tablespoons Curaçao
150 ml/¼ pint double cream
DECORATION
3 tablespoons chopped mixed nuts

Beat the chestnut purée with the finely grated rind of the orange
until very smooth. Stir in the icing sugar with the liqueur and 2
tablespoons of orange juice squeezed from the orange. Whip the
cream until stiff and fold through the chestnut purée mixture.
Then, whip the two mixtures together until thick enough to pipe.
 Spoon the mixture into a piping bag fitted with a large star nozzle.
Pipe into six tall glasses and chill well.
 Just before serving, scatter the chestnut whirls with the chopped
nuts. SERVES 6

Lemon
Cherry Chiffons

One of the easiest of whisked desserts, Lemon Chiffon is
made extra special by using liqueur-soaked cherries as a base.

350 g / 12 oz fresh dark red or black cherries
2 tablespoons cherry liqueur
3 eggs, separated
175 g / 6 oz castor sugar
2 lemons
1 tablespoon powdered gelatine
150 ml / ¼ pint whipping cream
DECORATION
mimosa balls
angelica

Stone the cherries and divide between six sundae glasses. Spoon a
little liqueur over each.

Place the egg yolks in a deep bowl, add the sugar and the finely
grated rind of both lemons and whisk until thick and creamy. Add
5 tablespoons of lemon juice from the two lemons. Dissolve the
gelatine in 3 tablespoons of boiling water and stir into the lemon
mixture.

Lightly whip the cream until it stands in soft peaks and stir into the
lemon mixture. Whisk the egg whites until very stiff and fold into
the lemon mixture making sure it is well blended. Spoon the
mixture over the cherries and refrigerate to set. Just before serving,
decorate with mimosa balls and angelica. SERVES 6

Strawberry Fool with Raspberry Sauce

A dessert to make when raspberries and strawberries are ripe and plentiful. To ring the changes, try the recipe in reverse: *Raspberry Fool with Strawberry Sauce* is just as delicious.

675 g / 1½ lb strawberries, puréed
75 g / 3 oz castor sugar
300 ml / ½ pint double cream
SAUCE
225 g / 8 oz raspberries
2 tablespoons castor sugar
1 tablespoon orange juice

Mix the strawberries with the castor sugar until well blended. Whip the cream until lightly thick and fold into the strawberry purée mixture. Spoon into six individual serving glasses and chill.

To make the sauce, blend the raspberries or pass through a fine sieve. Add the sugar and the orange juice and mix well. Serve each fool topped with a little of the raspberry sauce and crisp dessert biscuits. SERVES 6

Summer Pudding

Every traditional cuisine has its own way of using up
yesterdays bread, but none is more beguiling or delicious
than the British Summer Pudding – a chilled, scarlet
treat of raspberries, redcurrants or any other soft fruit in season.

450 g / 1 lb raspberries
450 g / 1 lb redcurrants
225 g / 8 oz castor sugar
6 tablespoons boiling water
12 thin slices bread, crusts removed
15 g / ½ oz butter

Wash and drain the fruit. Remove the stalks from the raspberries
and with a fork, pull the redcurrants from their stalks. Place in a
basin and add the sugar dissolved in the boiling water. Stir
thoroughly taking care not to bruise the fruit. Leave to stand for 15
minutes before straining off a few tablespoons of the resulting juice
to be used later.

Butter a 1-litre/1¾-pint pudding basin and line the bottom and
sides with the bread slices, trimming each slice to make a neat fit.
Reserve some pieces to make a lid.

Spoon the fruit into the bread-lined basin and cover with the
bread slices for the lid. Cover the pudding with a plate and put a
heavy weight on top to press the fruit down firmly. Chill in the
refrigerator for 8 hours or long enough for the juices to penetrate
and soak the bread.

To serve, turn out on to a serving dish. Spoon the reserved juice
over the pudding and serve alone or with fresh cream. SERVES 4–6

Whisky and Lemon Syllabub

Light and fluffy, this is the perfect dessert to serve
after a heavy main course. Serve with sponge fingers
or for special occasions, chocolate langues de chat.

1 lemon
6 tablespoons whisky
75 g / 3 oz castor sugar
300 ml / ½ pint double cream
25 g / 1 oz walnuts, finely chopped
25 g / 1 oz plain chocolate, grated
6 sponge fingers or chocolate langues de chat

Finely grate the lemon rind into the whisky in a deep bowl. Add the
sugar and leave to marinate for at least 15 minutes.

Lightly whip the cream and gradually whip into the whisky and
sugar mixture, keeping the cream stiff.

Carefully fold in the chopped walnuts and grated chocolate.
Spoon the mixture into six tall glasses and place a sponge finger or
chocolate langue de chat in each so that the fingers peep out above
the mixture. Chill for several hours before serving. SERVES 6

Mandarin Charlotte Russe

A splendid dessert to make the day before a party. If you do not have a Charlotte Russe mould, then use a 15-cm/6-inch cake tin.

1 (312-g/11-oz) can mandarin oranges
1 tablet lemon jelly
15 g/½ oz angelica, cut into diamonds
18 Boudoir biscuits
300 ml/½ pint whipping cream
2 tablespoons Orange Curaçao or Cointreau (optional)

Rinse a 600-ml/1-pint Charlotte Russe mould with cold water. Drain the fruit reserving the juice. Dissolve the jelly in 300 ml/½ pint boiling water and add the fruit syrup making the liquid up to 450 ml/¾ pint with water, if necessary.

Pour a thin layer of some of the liquid jelly into the bottom of the mould and put into the refrigerator to set.

Cut off one rounded end of each of the Boudoir biscuits so that they are 1.5 cm/½ inch shorter than the sides of the mould.

When the first layer of jelly is set, arrange some of the mandarin segments and angelica on it in an attractive pattern, dipping each piece in the reserved liquid jelly before you put them in place. Refrigerate until set. When the pattern is firm, cover it with another thin layer of some of the remaining liquid jelly and refrigerate. Meanwhile, whip the cream until fairly stiff and fold in the liqueur, if used.

When the jelly in the mould is firm, dip the sugared side of the biscuits, one at a time, in the reserved liquid jelly and stand them up, closely together, all round the sides of the mould, sugar side out. Fill the centre with alternate layers of whipped cream and mandarin segments, ending with cream.

Slowly spoon the remaining jelly down the sides of the mould between the biscuits; the liquid will be absorbed. When the jelly appears at the rim of the mould, chill the Charlotte Russe until required.

To serve, dip the mould in boiling water for about 15 seconds and unmould on to a serving plate. Decorate with any remaining cream and fruit, if liked. SERVES 6

Redcurrant Cheesecake

Cheesecakes are one of the simplest desserts to make in advance of a dinner party meal and can look so delicious if decorated with fresh fruit.

100 g/4 oz butter
225 g/8 oz digestive biscuits, crushed
1 teaspoon ground cinnamon
450 g/1 lb cream cheese
50 g/2 oz castor sugar
6 tablespoons single cream
575 g/1¼ lb redcurrants, topped and tailed
15 g/½ oz powdered gelatine
300 ml/½ pint double cream
1 egg white, stiffly whisked

Lightly grease a 23-cm/9-inch loose-bottomed cake tin with a little of the butter. Melt the remainder in a bowl over another bowl of hot water. In a medium mixing bowl, combine the crushed biscuits, the melted butter and the cinnamon. Line the base of the tin with this mixture using a metal spoon, pressing it firmly against the bottom. Set aside.

In a medium mixing bowl, beat the cream cheese and sugar together until smooth and creamy. Stir in the single cream and 450 g/1 lb of the redcurrants. Dissolve the gelatine in 2 tablespoons of boiling water and stir into the mixture. Spoon the mixture over the biscuit crust. Chill in the refrigerator for about 1 hour, until set.

Meanwhile, whip the double cream until it forms stiff peaks and fold in the stiffly whisked egg white.

Remove the cheesecake from the refrigerator and spoon the cream mixture over the top of the cheesecake, making swirling patterns with the back of the spoon.

Sprinkle the remaining redcurrants over the cream. Chill before serving. SERVES 6–8

Raspberry Meringue Gâteau

(Illustrated on page 95)

Meringues stay white and crisp if prepared the 'no-cook' way by drying them in a warm place such as an airing cupboard or boiler room instead of the oven. Sandwiched together with raspberry cream, meringue discs make a delicious dessert, special enough for a celebration meal.

oil for greasing
5 egg whites
275 g/10 oz castor sugar
450 ml/¾ pint double cream
1 (142-ml/5-fl oz) carton soured cream
450 g/1 lb raspberries

Prepare three baking trays by lining with greaseproof paper. Mark two 20-cm/8-inch circles on two of the trays for the meringue discs. Brush the paper on all the trays lightly with oil to prevent the meringue from sticking.

Whisk the egg whites until very stiff, add half the castor sugar and continue whisking until the meringue stands in stiff peaks. Finally fold in the remaining sugar.

Using two-thirds of the mixture, make the two meringue discs by spreading the meringue evenly and smoothly within the marked circles. Place the remaining meringue into a piping bag fitted with a plain nozzle and pipe small thumb-sized meringues on to the third baking tray until all the meringue mixture has been used. Place all the trays in a warm place, such as an airing cupboard, for about 48 hours until the meringue is dry and crisp. Stiffly whip 150 ml/¼ pint of the double cream with the soured cream. Fold in three-quarters of the raspberries and to use to sandwich the meringue discs together. Whip the remaining cream and spread some in a thin layer over the top and sides of the meringue. Press the small meringues around the edge of the dessert.

Pipe the remaining cream in a lattice effect over the top of the gâteau using a piping bag fitted with a plain nozzle. Decorate with the reserved raspberries. Eat on day of making. SERVES 10–12

Orange Posset

A super dinner party dessert that can be made well ahead.
For very special occasions, try substituting half of the
orange juice for an orange-flavoured liqueur such as Grand
Marnier or Cointreau.

600 ml / 1 pint double cream
1 teaspoon grated lemon peel
1 teaspoon grated orange peel
6 tablespoons dry white wine
3 tablespoons orange juice
2 tablespoons lemon juice
100 g / 4 oz castor sugar
3 egg whites
2 tablespoons castor sugar
GARNISH
orange rind cut in julienne strips
orange segments (optional)

Beat the cream, lemon peel and orange peel together in a large
bowl until stiff. Add the wine and beat again until thick. Gradually
add the orange and lemon juice with the 100 g / 4 oz sugar and beat
until the mixture is thick and creamy.

Whisk the egg whites in a small bowl until soft peaks form. Add
the 2 tablespoons sugar and whisk until the mixture is very stiff.
Fold in the orange cream mixture. Mound into a large serving dish
and chill for at least 30 minutes before serving. Serve garnished
with julienne strips of orange rind and orange segments, if used.
SERVES 4

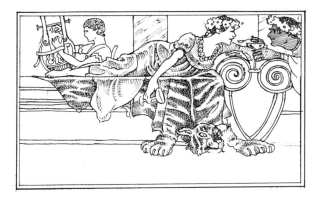

Biscuit Tortoni

During the 19th century, Tortoni's restaurant in Paris
was famous for its cold table. Victor Hugo, the famous
French novelist, often dined there and this ice cream
dessert is said to have been his favourite.

450 ml/¾ pint double cream
150 ml/¼ pint single cream
50 g/2 oz icing sugar
salt
12 macaroons
4½ tablespoons brown sherry
DECORATION
ratafia biscuits

If you do not have a freezer, turn the refrigerator ice making
compartment to its lowest setting about 1 hour before preparing
this dessert.

Whip the double and single cream together with the icing sugar
and a pinch of salt. When the mixture is firm but not too stiff, spoon
into a 23-cm/9-inch loaf tin and cover with a double layer of foil.
Freeze the cream until almost solid.

Put the macaroons into a plastic bag and crush to fine crumbs with
a rolling pin. Set aside one-third of the crumbs for decoration.

Turn the half-frozen cream mixture into a basin and blend the
sherry and the remaining two-thirds macaroon crumbs into the
mixture using a whisk. The mixture should stay light and bulky.
Return to the washed and dried loaf tin and freeze until solid.

When the cream has frozen quite solid again, remove the dish
from the freezer or refrigerator and invert on to a serving plate.
Press the reserved macaroon crumbs over the top and sides of the
ice cream block and serve, cut into thick slices, with ratafia biscuits.
SERVES 6–8

Cassata alla Siciliana

(Illustrated on page 95)

Sicily is famous for its extremely sweet and highly
coloured confectionery and crystallised fruits, and its
ice cream which is among the very best in the world. This
Cassata combines fruits and ice cream together and is
especially easy to make using ready prepared ice cream.

450 ml/¾ pint vanilla ice cream
300 ml/½ pint chocolate ice cream
150 ml/¼ pint double cream
50 g/2 oz icing sugar
100 g/4 oz crystallised fruits, diced
1 egg white

Using a metal spoon dipped in hot water, line the inside of a
1½-litre/2¾-pint pudding basin or mould with a layer of the vanilla
ice cream. Freeze until solid.

When solid, cover with a layer of chocolate ice cream making a
well in the centre for the final layer of cream. Freeze again until
solid.

Meanwhile, whip the cream until it stands in soft peaks and fold in
the icing sugar. Add the crystallised fruit and stir well to evenly
mix. Whisk the egg white until stiff and fold through the cream
mixture. Pile the mixture into the ice cream mould and smooth off
the top. Cover with foil and freeze again for several hours until the
whole Cassata is firm.

When ready to serve, dip the mould briefly in hot water and turn
the Cassata out on to a dish. Cut into wedges to serve. SERVES 8

Brown Bread Ice Cream

Based on a traditional English recipe and much more delicious than it sounds, this ice cream is best served with slightly under-sweetened summer fruits.

300 ml/½ pint double cream
150 ml/¼ pint single cream
75 g/3 oz icing sugar, sieved
100 g/4 oz brown breadcrumbs
1 tablespoon rum (optional)
2 eggs, separated

Whip the double cream until just stiff and gradually whisk in the single cream. Fold in the icing sugar and breadcrumbs. Lightly whisk the rum, if used, with the egg yolks and stir into the mixture. Whisk the egg whites until almost stiff and fold into the cream mixture. Pour the mixture into freezing trays or into a 1.2-litre/2-pint mould and freeze for about 3–4 hours until firm. SERVES 4–6

Khoshaf

(Illustrated on page 95)

Khoshaf is a Middle-Eastern fruit salad made of dried apricots and prunes, raisins and figs that are soaked in scented water for 2 days.

100 g/4 oz dried apricots
100 g/4 oz dried prunes, stones removed
100 g/4 oz seedless raisins
100 g/4 oz dried figs
1 tablespoon rose water or orange blossom water
50 g/2 oz flaked blanched almonds
25 g/1 oz split pistachio nuts

Put the apricots, prunes, raisins and figs in a large serving bowl. Pour in 600 ml/1 pint water and the rose water or orange blossom water. Leave the fruit to soak for at least two days, when the syrup will be rich and golden.
Serve sprinkled with the blanched almonds and pistachio nuts.
SERVES 4–6

Chocolate Mousse

This really is a long standing family favourite and it is so simple to make. The recipe can be made smaller or larger. All you have to remember is to allow 1 egg and 25 g/1 oz chocolate per person.

100 g/4 oz plain chocolate
15 g/½ oz butter
4 eggs
300 ml/½ pint double cream

Break the chocolate into small pieces and place in a bowl over another bowl of boiling water. Stir from time to time so that the chocolate melts. Stir in the butter, allow to melt and mix well.

Separate the eggs and add the yolks to the chocolate mixture, stirring well to blend.

Whisk the egg whites until stiff and fold through the chocolate mixture. Pour the mousse into individual serving dishes and chill to set. It is necessary to chill for several hours to achieve a firm texture. Serve the mousse with unwhipped double cream floating on top.

SERVES 4

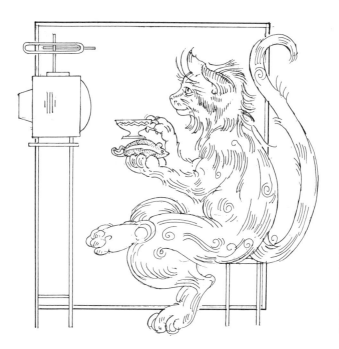

Coeur à la Crème

This is an attractive, light, classic French dessert. Coeur
à la Crème is often served with wild strawberries and sprinkled
with sugar but any fresh fruit may be used.

450 g/1 lb cream cheese
pinch of salt
300 ml/½ pint double cream
2 egg whites
2 tablespoons soft brown sugar

Gently rub the cream cheese and salt through a sieve into a large
mixing bowl. Beat with a wooden spoon until the mixture is
smooth. Gradually beat in the double cream.

Beat the egg whites until stiff and, with a metal spoon, fold into
the cream cheese mixture.

Line six Coeur à la Crème moulds with cheesecloth, or use six
small moulds with perforated bottoms. Spoon the cream cheese
mixture into the moulds. Leave the moulds to drain in the
refrigerator overnight or for at least 12 hours.

To serve, invert the moulds on to a serving dish, remove the
cheesecloth lining and scatter the crèmes with a little brown sugar.
Serve the Coeur à la Crèmes with extra double cream and soft
berry type fruits. SERVES 6

Chocolate Biscuit Gâteau

A real never-fail chocolate gâteau that is made from broken
pieces of biscuits, chocolate, eggs, butter and sugar. It
is the ideal dessert or cake to make when you get near
the bottom of the biscuit tin and find a few mis-shapen biscuits.

225 g/8 oz butter
2 eggs, beaten
25 g/1 oz castor sugar
225 g/8 oz plain chocolate
225 g/8 oz sweet biscuits, digestive, chocolate or gingernut biscuits
for example
DECORATION
150 ml/¼ pint double cream, whipped
glacé cherries
angelica

Grease a 15-cm/6-inch loose-bottomed cake tin. Place the butter in
a bowl over another bowl of boiling water and melt. Meanwhile,
beat the eggs with the sugar in another bowl and when thoroughly
combined, pour the melted butter into the mixture, beating
continuously. Melt the chocolate in a bowl over another bowl of
boiling water and add this to the butter mixture.

Break up the biscuits into small pieces and fold into the chocolate
mixture. Turn the mixture into the cake tin, smoothing the top
with a palette knife. Chill overnight in the refrigerator.

Push the cake out of the tin by loosening the base on to a serving
dish. Decorate with swirls of whipped cream, glacé cherries and
pieces of angelica. SERVES 6

Nuts

Whether whole or ground, roasted, chopped or caramelised, nuts are an indispensable part of both savoury and sweet cooking. Nuts provide integral flavouring and texture for ice creams, stuffings, sweets, biscuits, salads and garnishes.

Extremely rich in calories and nutrients, they have proved to be a valuable source of fat soluble vitamins and minerals as well as protein for vegetarians (especially vegans) and non-vegetarians alike. Added to salads, desserts and stuffings, they can literally transform a dish to new culinary heights. But remember, a little goes a long way so only buy the amount you intend to use quickly. Do not chop, grind or shell any more than you require for each recipe – nuts quickly lose their moisture and nutrients as well as flavour and crisp texture if left unused for too long.

Cheese and Walnut Dip

Walnuts combined with a mild cheese such as Wensleydale
makes a tasty and crunchy dip suitable to serve at a cocktail
party or informal buffet.

450 g / 1 lb Wensleydale or mild cheese
200 ml / 7 fl oz single cream
3 tablespoons milk
25 g / 1 oz onion, peeled and grated
tomato purée
salt and freshly ground black pepper
40 g / 1½ oz walnuts, finely chopped

Finely grate the cheese into a bowl. Add the cream and milk a little
at a time. Beat in the grated onion, tomato purée to taste and
seasoning. Finally fold in the chopped walnuts. Serve in a deep
bowl surrounded with chopped vegetables, crisps, crackers and
pretzels. MAKES 600 ml / 1 pint

Walnut Pairs

(Illustrated on page 96)

Walnut Pairs are walnuts sandwiched together with a piquant
cream cheese mixture. They make ideal savouries to go with
drinks but can also be packed away for a lunch box or picnic.

75 g / 3 oz full-fat soft cheese
onion salt
paprika
48 walnut halves (approximately 100 g / 4 oz)

Beat the cheese until soft and season to taste with onion salt and
paprika. Spread or pipe the cheese to sandwich the walnut halves
together. MAKES ABOUT 24

Frozen Hazelnut and Banana Yogurt

Frozen yogurt is an American invention and makes a delightful alternative to ice cream. Serve as a delicious low-calorie dessert or snack or even breakfast-time treat.

4 medium bananas
1 lemon
1–2 tablespoons rum
300 ml/½ pint natural yogurt
2 tablespoons soft brown sugar
2 egg whites
50 g/2 oz roasted hazelnuts, chopped

Peel the bananas, place in a bowl and mash well with a fork. Beat in the grated rind and juice of the lemon and the rum. Add the yogurt and brown sugar and mix well.

Whisk the egg whites until stiff then fold into the banana mixture. Put the bowl into the freezer or ice-making compartment of the refrigerator and freeze until the mixture is half-frozen.

Remove from the freezer and whisk well. Stir in the chopped hazelnuts and return to the freezer to freeze again, until half solid. Remove and stir again to mix well, taking care not to break up the nuts. Spoon into a rigid container and freeze until solid. Serve in scoops. SERVES 4

Brazil Nut Salad

A nourishing first course, light lunch dish or hearty snack, Brazil Nut Salad combines the smoothness of bananas with the crunchiness of Brazil nuts.

1 crisp head of lettuce, washed and separated into leaves
3 tablespoons Vinaigrette Dressing (see page 59)
3 bananas
1 tablespoon lemon juice
100 g / 4 oz Brazil nuts, finely chopped

Arrange half the lettuce leaves in a shallow serving bowl. Set aside.
Shred the remaining lettuce into a mixing bowl. Pour over the dressing and toss the lettuce until it is well coated.

Peel the bananas and slice them into a small mixing bowl. Sprinkle over the lemon juice. Add half of the sliced bananas and all the Brazil nuts to the shredded lettuce and toss the ingredients together.

Pile the nut and banana mixture on top of the lettuce-lined serving bowl. Arrange the remaining banana slices around the edge in a ring. Serve immediately. SERVES 4

Pecan Peach Salad

This salad is best prepared during the summer months when fresh peaches are in abundant supply. To peel, immerse the peaches in boiling water for a few seconds to loosen the skins.

4 ripe peaches, peeled, halved and stoned
2 tablespoons lemon juice
225 g/8 oz cottage cheese
100 g/4 oz pecan nuts, finely chopped
8 lettuce leaves

Put the peaches in a mixing bowl and sprinkle with the lemon juice. Toss until well coated.

Mix together the cottage cheese, pecan nuts and any drained lemon juice. Arrange the lettuce leaves on four individual serving dishes. Place two peach halves on each dish, cut sides up. Spoon the cottage cheese mixture into the centres and serve. SERVES 4

Apple, Cashew and Celeriac Crunch

This is a substantial side salad type dish of the above ingredients. Make just before serving to prevent the apples from turning brown.

675 g / 1½ lb celeriac
5 tablespoons mayonnaise
1 teaspoon salt
1 tablespoon finely chopped fresh chervil or borage
1 tablespoon finely chopped parsley
2 crisp eating apples, cored and thinly sliced into rings
100 g / 4 oz salted cashew nuts, finely chopped

Slice the celeriac very thinly into paper-thin slices. Mix the mayonnaise, salt, chervil or borage and parsley together. Add the apple and celeriac slices and stir to coat. Place on a serving dish and sprinkle with the nuts before serving. SERVES 4

Nut and Sultana Bars

(Illustrated on page 96)

These no-cook biscuits are tempting treats for adults
and children alike. Wrap in foil for picnics and alfresco
meals or as a special treat for schoolchildren's lunch box.

100 g/4 oz digestive biscuits
50 g/2 oz plain sweet biscuits
75 g/3 oz sultanas
75 g/3 oz walnuts, chopped
2 tablespoons golden syrup
75 g/3 oz butter
50 g/2 oz plain chocolate

Grease a shallow 18-cm/7-inch square tin. Put all the biscuits in a
polythene bag and crush with a rolling pin. Put into a bowl and mix
in the sultanas and walnuts.

Place the golden syrup, butter and chocolate in a small bowl over
another bowl of boiling water and stir until the mixture has melted
and is well combined. Pour on to the biscuit, fruit and nut mixture
and mix well to combine. Spoon into the prepared tin and smooth
with a palette knife. Chill until set. Use a hot wet knife to cut into
bars before serving. MAKES 12 bars

Hazelnut Truffles

(Illustrated on page 96)

These scrumptious after dinner type sweets are best eaten on the day of making but will keep for a few days if stored in an air-tight container in the refrigerator.

50 g/2 oz hazelnuts
50 g/2 oz unsalted butter
100 g/4 oz breakfast oats
100 g/4 oz castor sugar
2–3 tablespoons melted chocolate or cocoa powder
rum essence
3–4 tablespoons black coffee

Rub the skins off the nuts. Beat the butter until soft and work in the oats, sugar and chocolate or cocoa powder until well blended. Add a few drops of rum essence and enough coffee to bind the mixture without making it sticky.

Leave the mixture in a cool place to firm slightly then divide into small pieces and shape into round balls. Set a hazelnut on top of each ball and press down lightly. Alternatively, chop the nuts finely and use to coat the balls. Place in sweet cases and serve. MAKES ABOUT 20

Index